Connections

ADVANCED
Student Edition

Dorothy Woods

English Anywhere Inc.
6513 Patricia Avenue
Plano, Texas 75023

www.englishanywhere.org

copyright 2009
Printed in the United States of America

All rights reserved: no part of this publication may be reproduced, stored in a retrieval system, or transmitted, in any form or by any means electronic, mechanical, photocopying, recording, or otherwise without the prior written permission of the Publisher.

The Publisher grants permission for the photocopying of these pages according to the following conditions. Individual purchasers may make copies for their own use or for use by classes they teach. School or church purchasers may make copies for use by their staff and students, but this permission does not extend to additional schools or churches. Under no circumstamces may any part of this book be photocopied for resale.

ISBN-13: 978-1517205881

ISBN-10: 1517205883

Acknowledgements

As the need for speaking English becomes a world wide necessity, the teachers of English are faced with many choices for good curriculum. These lessons are the basic knowledge that students need to begin their acquisition of the English language. Our goal is to provide a structured textbook that can be used by teachers and students to accomplish the skills necessary to speak English as a native speaker. The lessons are designed to aid the student in the spoken language and assume that they have already mastered some of the reading and writing skills taught in many schools around the world.

We have incorporated the most current teaching techniques for acquiring a language, and use many activities to aid in practicing the skills taught in each lesson. In Lesson 12 we included a story and use Penny Hiller's Story Approach to teach the skills needed in that lesson. We have employed the basic concepts of Gardner's *Theory of Multiple Intelligences* to reach the widest range of student's learning, and we hope you will enjoy teaching these lessons.

Special thanks to:

Gloria Ormiston for field testing these lessons in Enable Learning Center in Minneapolis, Minnesota and in the church in Bangkok, Thailand.

Ed Woods for the many hours of contributions and help with these lessons at Enable Learning Center in Minneapolis, Minnesota.

All of our friends and families who have given their financial, prayer, and spiritual support throughtout the long process of writing and field testing this curriculum.

Dedication

To my husband, Ed Woods, who is my
cheerleader, prompter, co-worker, best friend,
godly example, and knight in shining armor.

And to our children and their families
who have encouraged and endured me
during the writing of this text.

About the Author

Dorothy A. Woods has served with her husband, Edward, as church planters with Continental Baptist Missions since 1970. Dorothy has a graduate degree in education and a wide variety of teaching experience. Since 1994 the Lord has privileged Ed and Dorothy to focus on ESL (English as a Second Language) as an outreach of the local church. They have conducted tutor training workshops in churches, Bible colleges, and mission agencies in the US, Canada, and overseas. Currently the Woods are living in New York, where they each ESL through the ENABLE Learning Center to Hmong refugees, assist international students at the University of Minnesota, and continue to challenge and equip Christians for Great Commission living. The Woods have three grown children and three grandsons.

Idiom illustrations drawn by Holly Minniear while she was a busy art student.

Contributing Editor: Suzanne Carter, Director of English Anywhere, Inc.

Chapter Order

	Each chapter will include the following components:	**Type of Learner**

 Theme picture with a question or quote   VISUAL

 Conversation: small group or class conversation centering around the theme   INTERPERSONAL

 Social Situations: understanding and practicing common social skills,   INTERPERSONAL

 Pronunciation: individual problem areas, stress, intonation.   LINGUISTIC

 Perception: idioms in context, American culture and values   VISUAL

 **Listening and Bible Knowledge**: listening skills tips, listening to Bible content, songs, hymns   MUSICAL

 **Discussion**: questions about Bible content and the chapter theme   LOGICAL

 **Assignment:** reading, writing, options to improve problem areas, drawing, composing   INTERAPERSONAL

    KENESTHETIC

Some of the following will also be include:

Role play
Questions for discussion and/or writing
Research and presentation
Personal application
Chain story
Concept maps
Oral exercises
Dictation
Creative writing, drawing, composing
Problem solving
Songs, folk songs, ballads, hymns

Segment of the lessons

A. THEME PICTURE

1) Purpose
   a) to focus thinking on the theme subject, to warm up to the subject and to discover prior knowledge.
2) Procedure
   a) Look together at the picture and question, and think and respond to the question.
   b) connect the questions with the theme.
   c) Give responses and opinions.
3) Possible activities
   a) Include other pictures about the same theme to expand thinking and connectivity.

B. CONVERSATIONS

1) Purpose
   a) To delve into the subject of the lesson in greater detail, to move from abstract to concrete

2) Procedure
   a) If the class is large, break into pairs and discuss the questions.
   b) If the class is small, stay together to discuss.
   c) Read the questions aloud, clarifying if needed.
   d) Take notes if you so desire.
3) Possible activities
   a) Illustrate pertinent concepts on the board.
   b) Ask questions and expand of the conversation.

C. SOCIAL SITUATIONS

1) Purpose
   a) To develop confidence in facing various common social situations
   b) To explore American customs and traditions
   c) To create awareness of sensitive issues and suggest responses
2) Procedure
   a) Usually stay together as a whole class unless otherwise specified
   b) Take turns reading aloud
   c) Teacher fill in any necessary information
   d) Allow time for questions about the situation
   e) Break into pairs and practice when appropriate
3) Possible activities
   a) Model the situation with another classmate then discuss it
   b) Role play a similar situation
   c) Write a scene depicting a similar situation
   d) Use photos, DVDs, or other media to expand on the subject
      example: wedding album, wedding music, reception favors

G. LISTENING and BIBLE KNOWLEDGE
1) Purpose
    a) To improve listening skills by developing awareness of speech habits
    b) To employ listening tactics such as reductions and linking
    c) To familiarize yourself with God's eternal redemptive plan
2) Procedure
    a) For listening tips and Bible Introduction:
        (1) Either play the CD or have the teacher read the entire selection.
        (2) Read again, but in sections, with time to clarify and answer questions, take notes or underline unclear parts.
        (3) Listen again, focusing on main ideas, on details, or on some other feature.
3) Possible activities
    a) Use a Bible in your native language
    b) Divide into language groups and read in your heart language, then in English.
    c) Together as a class, view the corresponding portion of "God's Story" or "The Hope" DVD.

H. DISCUSSION

1) Purpose
    a) To clarify content of Bible selection
    b) To provide opportunities for questions
2) Procedure
    a) Stay together as a class.
    b) Read each question. Then discuss it.
    c) Field other questions.
    d) Read the Bible story in your native language on your own
3) Possible activities
    a) Introduce appropriate visuals to clarify and visualize concepts.
        (ex. "library" of the books of the Bible)
    b) Dramatize the Bible account.
    c) Songs or hymns that reflect the Bible selection or topic .

I. ASSIGNMENT
1) Purpose
    a) To internalize skills, information, spiritual lessons
    b) To create opportunities to reflect on and expand on knowledge
    c) To use what you have learned
    d) To provide a venue for spiritual life, growth, and change
2) Procedure
    a) Read options. Ask the teacher to clarify as needed.
    b) Try to do at least one option.
    c) Present your assignment at the next class session.
3) Possible activities
    a) Encourage creativity—painting, sketching, composing, creative writing.
    b) Encourage sharing
    c) Appreciate God given talents

Suggested resources for Listening:
1. Feinstein, Gail. It All Started in Kindergarten:
   Book: ISBN 0-13-630971-2; Cassettes: ISBN 0-13-631011-7
2. Numrice, Carol. Face the Issues: (National Public Radio interviews)
   Book: ISBN 0-201-84672-1; Cassettes: ISBN 0-201-69518-9
3. Fragiadakis, Helen. All Clear! Advanced Idioms in Context:
   Book: ISBN 0-8384-4721-X, Tapes(2) ISBN 0-8384-4722-8
4. Mendelsohn, David. Learning to Listen: A Strategy Based Approach for the Second Language Learner. ISBN 1-56270-299-8
5. TV shows that you enjoy; especially the News broadcasts

Suggested resources for Conversations:
1. Fragiadakis, Helen Kalkstein. All Clear! Advanced Idioms and Pronunciation In Context . Book ISBN 0-8384-4721-X. Cassettes:ISBN 0-8384-4722-8
2. Kehe, David and Peggy. Conversation Strategies. ISBN 0-86647-08-4
3. Graham, Carolyn. Small Talk. Text ISBN 0-19-434220-4
4. Rucinski-Hatch. The Journal of the Imagination in Language Learning and Teaching, Volume 111. "Grandma Moses Meets ESL: Art for Speaking and Writing Activities." www.njcu.edu/cill/vol3rucinski-hatch.html
5. Hancock, Mark. Pronunciation Games. ISBN 0-521-46735-7
6. Althen, Gary. American Ways: A Guide for Foreigners in the United States. ISBN 0-933662-68-8

Suggested Resources for Pronunciation:
1. Sudlow, Michael. Exercises in American English Pronunciation.
   Text ISBN 1-877591-21-1

Suggested Resources for Specific Purpose English:
1. Barron's: Essential Words for the TOEFL. ISBN 0-8120-1470-7
2. Hemmert, Amy and O'Connell, Ged. Communicating on Campus: Skills for Academic Speaking. ISBN: 1-882483-67-7
3. Numrich, Carol. Face the Issues. National Public Radio.
   Text ISBN: 0-201-84672-1. Cassettes ISBN: 0-201-69518-9

Student Book

Table of Contents

Chapter 1	Foundations	4
Chapter 2	Creation and Time	14
Chapter 3	Relationships and Ruin	26
Chapter 4	Catastrophes	38
Chapter 5	United Nations?	50
Chapter 6	A Mobile World	60
Chapter 7	Leadership	70
Chapter 8	Justice	82
Chapter 9	Worries, Fears, and Promises	92
Chapter 10	Hope Arrives	102
Chapter 11	Amazing Accomplishments	114
Chapter 12	The Master Teacher	126
Chapter 13	Parades, Plots, and Problems	138
Chapter 14	Tragedy or Triumph	150
Chapter 15	The Future	165

July 4, 1776 painting by John Trumbull.

The Declaration of Independence

Chapter 1: Foundations
What do these pictures have in common?

Conversations: Foundations

1. What is a foundation?

2. In addition to buildings, what else has a foundation?

3. What are the purposes of a foundation?

4. What influences the type of foundation someone builds?

5. Before constructing a foundation, what must be done?

6. Do any of these steps apply to other types of foundations? How?

Social Situations: Meeting People

In your new surroundings you will meet many people. What should you say when someone introduces you to a stranger? How can you avoid embarrassment?

1. Introductions
    a. What have you noticed about the nature of introductions? Are they formal or informal? Give examples and practice both styles.

    b. Who is mentioned first in the introduction? Is this consistent? Is it important?

    c. How does this compare/contrast with introductions in your native language?

2. Small Talk
    a. Most westerners (Americans, anyway) seem to spend a lot of time with "small talk," subjects that do not seem important. What subjects have you noticed usually are part of this small talk?

    b. Is this a common practice in your language?

    c. Do you think it is useful or a waste of time? Why?

3. Subjects to avoid
    Train yourself to notice what subjects are taboo (not appropriate) for introductory conversations. List some below. Then try to avoid them—at least until you know someone fairly well.

Pronunciation

Reductions: Contractions are an integral part of English speech. Whether or not you like them, you must learn to understand them; and if you want to sound like a native English speaker, incorporate contractions into your own speech. Here are a few basic contractions to master.

1. Simple present of verb to be

<u>Singular</u>

I am	I'm
you are	you're
he is	he's
she is	she's
it is	it's

<u>Plural</u>

we are	we're
you are	you're
they are	they're

<u>Negative singular</u>

I am not	I'm not	I'm not
you are not	you're not	you aren't
he is not	he's not	he isn't
she is not	she's not	she isn't
it is not	it's not	it isn't

<u>Negative plural</u>

we are not	we're not	we aren't
you are not	you're not	you aren't
they are not	they're not	they aren't

Get with a partner and practice listening to and saying these basic contractions.

2. A name followed by *is*:
   When a name is followed by the verb *is*, the *i* in *is* is dropped and the z sound is added to the name. Examples:

   Brad's a hard worker.
   Sue's a second grade teacher.
   Kenji's a well known scholar.
   Keeko's a cheerful person.

   Read these sentences aloud, concentrating on the reduction. Then compose some practice sentences of your own.

Pronunciation Problems

There are many sounds in the English language that are typically difficult for language learners to master. Listen as your teacher says each word; then repeat it. Find a partner and practice these lists. You may not conquer these troublesome sounds immediately, but if you work on them, you can improve your speaking skills.

t/th		p/f	
ten	then	pat	fat
tear	there	pad	fad
tan	than	pill	fill
tease	these	pony	phony
toes	those	cap	calf
toe	though	paint	faint
		pig	fig

Perception: Idioms and Phrasals, Culture Clues

Listen to the following dialogue and underline any idioms or phrases that are unfamiliar to you.

Sam: I have a problem and I really need your opinion.

Brad: **Fire away!** I have time to listen.

Sam: Well, as CEO of "Tons of Tools," I'm very concerned about some of our employees. They have little interest in developing their "people skills," especially with internationals. I've usually **hit it off** well with my overseas contacts, but the others seem totally ignorant of proper dealings with people from different cultures. I feel like I'm **hitting my head against a brick wall.**

Brad: Sam, keep in mind that people from small towns have limited contact with people of diverse cultural backgrounds. So this isn't surprising. Maybe you could consider writing a handout, "The **Nuts and Bolts** of International Business Dealings," or something like that.

Sam: I've been **hammering away** at attitude changes, but it hasn't helped much. Maybe I need to be more direct—**shake my employees to their foundations!** Maybe I should propose a mandatory trip overseas or a mandatory course on cross-cultural communication. These people are SO ethnocentric!

Brad: Do you ever conduct in-service training? Perhaps that would be more practical than sending each person overseas. If you start with your own experiences and build on your success, maybe you can **hammer home** the importance of respect and awareness of cultural differences in business dealings.

Sam: In-service training! **You hit the nail on the head!** That's a great idea! If we start there and build cultural awareness into our monthly team meetings, maybe we can **hammer some sense into** these guys.

Brad: If "Tons of Tools" plans to **build bridges** with overseas suppliers, you have to **build up** personal knowledge and awareness among your employees. Even though they might not travel themselves, **seeing the big picture** of the company's future might make them more receptive. Who knows when some **big shot** from China or elsewhere might walk through your doors? The employees need to become global thinkers instead of **small-towners**.

Sam: Thanks for your input. I think we're **onto something** here.

New expressions: Idioms and Phrasals

1. What do you think these might mean? How can you use them in your own conversations?
    a. Fire away!
    b. hit it off
    c. hitting my head against a brick wall
    d. the nuts and bolts
    e. hammer away at

    f. shake something to its foundations

    g. hammer home
    h. hit the nail on the head
    i. hammer some sense into
    j. build bridges

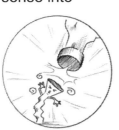

    k. the big picture
    l. big shot
    m small-towner
    n. onto something

Culture Clues: Individualism and Equality

The history of the United States provides a basis for understanding some of the cultural patterns that are woven into the fabric of American lives. Many of the first European settlers were part of groups born of the Protestant Reformation in Europe. They firmly supported the concepts of individual responsibility to God, freedom of conscience, and the equality of all humans, though they did not necessarily follow those teachings consistently.

Individualism and equality contrasted with the presence of a ruling class and a working class in most countries. Rugged individualism formed part of the young country's strength and enabled people to dare, to risk, and to attempt otherwise unheard of tasks. Robert Fulton's Erie Canal in New York State is an example.

Often today in America, the rights of individuals seem to be more important than family or parental input in decision-making. "I have a right," in its extreme, sometimes results in self-centeredness, egotism, and ethnocentrism.

1. If you've watched any TV or movie police stories, you've probably seen an officer "reading rights" to a suspect being arrested. The officer must read this Miranda warning:
    "You have the right to remain silent. Anything you say can and will be used against you in a court of law. You have the right to speak to an attorney, and to have an attorney present during any questioning. If you cannot afford a lawyer, one will be provided for you at government expense."
    a. Do you think this is fair? Why or why not?
    b. Have you ever had a confrontation with the law here? What happened?
2. In the US Declaration of Independence are these words: "We hold these truths to be self-evident, that all men are created equal, that they are endowed by their Creator with certain unalienable rights, that among these are life, liberty, and the pursuit of happiness."
    a. As you have observed life here, would you say that you've seen equality or inequality most often? In what situations?
    b. Look for cartoons about individualism or equality and share them in our next class.
    c. Create a skit showing how people treat each other equally— or unequally.

Listening and Bible Knowledge

This section begins tips on listening effectively to English as well as an overview of the Bible, the book that has tremendously influenced western culture.

Non-native speakers often complain about the speed at which others speak. Here are some suggestions on overcoming this bump along your language road.

      a. Politely tell the speaker that English is not your first language and ask the person to speak more slowly.

      b. Try to focus on the content words, not the fillers. What are some fillers that you often hear?

Bible Knowledge

Part 1: Introduction to the Bible

Listen to the CD or to your teacher reading an article entitled "The Bible: Foundation for Christian Belief." Focus on content words and main concepts rather than details. If it helps, take notes while listening. Obviously you won't be able to do this in a social situation, but it many help train your ear to listen for the most important ideas in a conversation, a song, or a video.

The Bible: Foundation for Christianity

"The familiar observation that the Bible is the best-selling book of all time obscures a more startling fact: The Bible is the best-selling book of the year, every year."* Why is it that a book written centuries ago bears this distinction? Why do men, women, and children from every nation and walk of life read this book? Why is its message the foundation of Christian thought and practice?

The Bible, also called The Holy Bible, is a unique book. Someone has stated, "The Bible is not such a book as man would write if he could, or could write if he would." It is a compilation of writings by more than 40 human writers, written in three languages on three continents over 1600 years. Despite these factors, its message is a unified presentation of God, creation, man, sin, history, deliverance, and future events. It explains God as creator, giver and preserver of life; one who is all powerful and all knowing; one whose eyes see everything. He is holy and perfect in every way.

The Bible also explains humans as created perfect; yet now they are selfish, sinful, and separated from God. It tells of God's mercy and grace in providing a way to re-establish man's relationship to God through the sacrifice of the Lord Jesus Christ, God's Promised Deliverer and Savior.

Discussion: Part 1

Think about the article's content as you discuss these questions.

1. Why do you think the Bible is the best selling book?
2. Why is the Bible considered a unique book?
3. What does the Bible explain?

Part 2: Introduction to the Bible

The message of the Bible has transformed lives and transcended culture. It has changed men like John Newton from slave trader to writer of "Amazing Grace." It has influenced Parliamentarian William Wilberforce to put his career in jeopardy to battle England's slave trade. It has moved men like William Carey, Hudson Taylor, and Adoniram Judson from comfortable lives to lives of simplicity, danger, and sacrifice on faraway continents so that others could learn the Bible's message and its transforming power.

History and science have affirmed the Bible's accuracy and veracity. Numberless followers of its teaching have given their lives to preserve its very existence. Governments have banned it, burned it, jailed its followers, and even burned them. Yet the Bible has survived and thrived through the centuries. It has inspired poets, musicians, and artists whose works reflect its message.

Individuals have found within its pages wisdom for daily life, encouragement in times of distress, guidance for personal behavior. The Bible offers hope, peace, forgiveness, and a vital relationship with the Creator God. The Bible transcends cultures, time, gender, economic status. It remains the best seller because it truly transforms lives. Is it not worth reading?

www.newyorker.com/archive/2006/12/18/061218fact1)

Discussion: Part 2

Think about the article's content as you discuss these questions.

1. Why do you think the Bible has changed so many lives?
2. How has it influenced lives? Name some people mentioned in the article.
3. In what ways has the Bible been attacked? Have these attacks succeeded?
4. What does the Bible offer?

 # Assignment

Choose at least one of the following and be prepared to share in class.

1. Write questions you have about "The Bible: Foundation for Christianity."

2. Someone wrote, "Individualism can be seen as a gift or a curse, depending on the context in which it occurs." In your opinion, when can it be a curse, and when can it be a gift?

3. Select one of the men mentioned in the article and research his life and contribution to society. Write a summary to share in class.

4. Watch the movie (DVD) "Amazing Grace" and note how the Bible influenced William Wilberforce's driving life passion.

5. Have you ever read the Bible?
    What are your reactions to it?
    Would you be interested in studying it in greater detail?

6. Look for a song about the Bible and bring a copy to class. If you are able, plan to sing it to or with the class.

7. In your country, is the Bible commonly accepted as a holy book? Why or why not? Is there another book that strongly influences your culture?

8. Write an essay comparing and contrasting individualism and equality in the USA with that in your home country.

9. Draw a cartoon or picture depicting the concepts of individuality and/or equality. Prepare to share it with the class.

The "Hudson River School" of artists

Chapter 2: Creation and Time
How did these things come into existence?

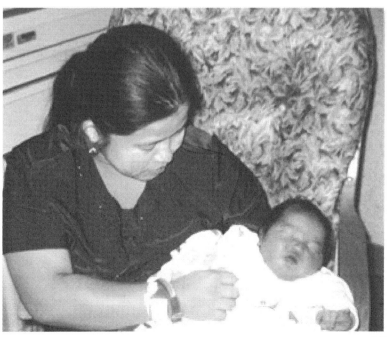

Conversation: Creating something

1. Have you ever created something? Perhaps a game, a toy, a model? Tell about it. Why did you make it? What was its purpose? How long did it take to make it? What tools did you use? Do you still have it?

2. What are the differences between the words create, make, and develop?

3. What does a creation indicate about its creator?

4. Describe the most beautiful thing you have seen in the natural world. Be as specific as possible.

Social Situations: Creating friendships

In order to feel "at home" in your new setting, it is important to develop new friendships. How can you get to know someone? Should you take the initiative, or wait for the other person to start a conversation which may develop into a friendship?

1. Taking the initiative
    *Think of the activities and interests you already have. List them.

    *Think of some new things you'd like to know more about while you're here. List them.

2. Where might you find people who share your interests?

3. This week make an effort to talk with someone new or to further develop a relationship with someone you've met since moving here. Be prepared to share what happens.

Pronunciation

Past tense verbs are sometimes puzzling. Do you pronounce them with an extra syllable, with a t, or with a d sound? There are some guidelines that actually work!

Past tense verbs that end with a d or t require the addition of an extra syllable—**ed**. Practice these examples from this lesson, first by yourself, then with a partner.

create	created	divide	divided
wait	waited	rest	rested
indicate	indicated	reflect	reflected
suggest	suggested	commit	committed
exist	existed	substitute	substituted

If this is a problem for you, make an ongoing list in your notebook of verbs and past tenses. Then regularly practice saying them aloud.

Pronunciation problems

Small differences in English sounds are difficult for language learners to distinguish and pronounce. Listen as the teacher says each word pair; then repeat each word. Now get with a partner. While one says a word from each pair, the other circles it with pencil. After you've checked your work, switch roles and do it again.

w/v

a. went   vent   d. grow   grove   g. wet   vet

b. wow   vow   e. wiser visor   h. worse verse

c. west   vest   f. wine   vine   i. wail   veil

List some of the English sounds that cause you trouble. Work with your teacher or a partner to read the words with that sound. Then practice pronouncing them correctly.

Perception: Idioms, phrasals, culture clues

Idioms and phrasals are problematic features of English speech, especially since they are so frequently used. While you may know the literal meaning of each word, the combinations are confusing. Phrasals refer to combinations of verbs and prepositions to indicate meaning.

Listen to the following dialogue and underline any idioms or phrases that are unfamiliar to you.

Pam: I am really upset! Cathy just **makes my blood boil!**

Mark: Whoa! Calm down! What happened?

Pam: We have a major project due next Friday, but two of our team members are sick. Since **time is money**, I suggested that we **make the best of the situation**, and continue working. But now Cathy doesn't want to.

Mark: Why not? You need to **make the most of your time** even without the others.

Pam: I agree. But here's what happened. I **took time off** from my job in order to meet with Cathy. On my way to our meeting, I stopped for coffee and ran into an old friend. Well, **time got away from me**, and I was an hour late for the meeting.

Mark: I think you make Cathy's blood boil! **Make up your mind**. Are you going to work as a team or not? I know **time flies when you're having fun**, but you have a responsibility. I think you owe Cathy an apology.

Pam: Well, maybe you're right. Somehow I need to **make up for** my carelessness. What do you suggest?

Mark: **Take time to catch your breath**. Then go tell Cathy what happened. She'll probably understand. Maybe you can still **make a go of it**. After all, **time heals all wounds.**

New Expressions: Idioms and Phrasals

What do you think these might mean? How can you use them in your own conversations?

a. makes my blood boil
b. Time is money.

c. Make the best of the situation.
d. make the most of your time
e. took time off
f. Time got away from me.

g. Make up your mind.
h. Time flies when you're having fun.
i. make up for

j. Take time to catch your breath.
k. make a go of it
l. Time heals all wounds.

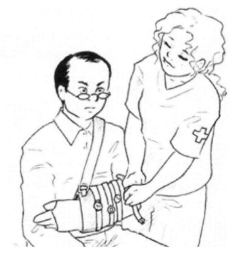

If you go to www.wordpower.ws/idioms/m, you will find many more phrases using the word make. Look over this list and bring your questions to class next time.

Culture Clues: Time

a. Read the following; then answer the question that follows.

You are a secretary in a doctor's office. A man rushes in, checking his watch. He checks in with you. You notice the time is 2:05. His appointment is scheduled for 2:00. he sits down, picks up a magazine, and begins flipping through it. At 2:15 you see him check his watch again and look at the door that leads to the check-up offices. Five minutes later, you see him shifting in his seat and looking at his watch again. You notice him again looking at his watch and glancing at the door. He does not have a very pleasant look on his face. Ten minutes later, this man puts down the magazine and angrily walks out of the doctor's office. Why?

1. He is scared and nervous about his appointment so he leaves, unable to handle his fear anymore.
2. He was offended by something he read in the magazine.
3. He was offended by having to wait so long to see the doctor.
4. He was uncomfortable sitting in the office with other people.

(from www.linguistics.byu.edu/resources/lp/lpc2)

b. Have you observed similar situations? Describe them to your partner, then prepare to role play a situation about time to the whole class. (Possibilities: an office, a party, a class, a meeting, a date) Write your ideas.

c. If you have come from an eastern culture or a Latino/Hispanic culture, you have probably noticed that time is a big issue here. People are often checking their watches, asking others what time something is scheduled, and worrying about time. Control of time seems very important to many native English speakers. Being on time, time management, and setting goals (both immediate and long-term), are important to many Americans.

Sit with another classmate and discuss the following:

1. What have you noticed about people's apparent preoccupation with time?
2. Contrast or compare this with your homeland.
3. Can you think of adjustments you should make in order to fit into this time-oriented society?

Listening and Bible Knowledge

Listening tips: Reductions

Native English speakers usually do not pronounce every sound in a word, or even every word distinctly. Train your ear to listen for the content rather than the individual word or sound. If you want to sound like a native English speaker, practice these reductions and intentionally employ them in your conversations this week.

a. **going to** (+ a verb): Becomes **gunna**.

    1) He's going to study late tonight.
    2) Where are you going to eat after class?
    3) My parents are going to be proud of my good grades.
    4) Luke and Lisa are going to get married next month.
    5) We're going to prepare Chinese food Friday night.
    6) Write your own sentence using going to; then read it as a reduction.

b. **kind of / sort of** becomes *kinda, kina, sorda*

    1) He's kind of tired after studying all night.
    2) What kind of soup is your favorite?
    3) Ben is sort of grouchy today. I wonder why.
    4) A pit bull is kind of dangerous if it gets upset.
    5) I don't know what kind of person would ignore that accident.
    6) Write your own sentences using kind of and sort of ; then read aloud.

Bible Knowledge

This section will begin an overview of the Bible, which forms the basis of western civilization. Though some individuals and governments do not often consider the Bible's teaching, the Bible is still important in understanding western culture and thought.

Many individuals and churches take the Bible very seriously, and find guidance and instruction for practical aspects of daily life. There is insufficient time and space in this curriculum to give detailed attention to the entire Bible. Rather, we will consider the "meta-narrative," (the big picture or the main story) in order to understand who God is, what He has done, and what He has planned for the future.

The best place to start is at the beginning: CREATION Please listen as your teacher reads a summary of the creation. (or listen to the CD). Feel free to take notes, especially of words or phrases you do not understand. Then listen again, and enjoy the discussion of this very intriguing and important subject.

Part 1: God and Creation

According to the Bible, this is how the world came into being. Before there was anything that we can see in this universe, God existed. He is the eternal, self-existent creator of all things. He has no beginning and no ending. He does not need the help of any person or thing in order to exist.

God is Spirit which means He has no physical appearance unless He chooses to reveal Himself to man. He is also personal, caring about His creation and appearing to man in personal ways through His Visible Image.

This One True God created the earth, the sky, the seas, the planets, the stars, the galaxies, and moons, as well as all living things. He established time through His orderly arrangement of everything. Because He made everything, He owns everything. He is the Supreme Ruler over all of creation. He and His creation are on different levels, and are not equal.

The One True God, Supreme Ruler of all, created the entire natural world in six days. First He formed the world, then He filled it. God spoke and there was light. He separated the light from the darkness and produced "day and night," on the **first day**. On the **second day**, God spoke and divided the deep waters that covered the earth. He made a place for the seas and an atmosphere for the sky. On the **third day**, God spoke and dry land appeared out of the waters of the earth. He also created great numbers of plants and trees to grow on the land. God made the sun, the moon, and the stars on the **fourth day**. On the **fifth day**. He created many species of sea creatures to inhabit the water and birds to fly in the air. On the **sixth day**, God made all creatures that live on the land: animals, reptiles, insects, and every living thing. He also created man.

God spoke all these things into existence. He created them from nothing, and He created them to live in harmony with one another. All that God created was good.

On the seventh day, God rested. This was not because He was tired, but to teach man of his need to reserve a special day for rest and reflection on God, his Creator. God wants man to consider all that God is and does, and to worship Him, the One True Creator.

Discussion: Part 1

1. What does it mean when we say God is self-existent?
2. How many days did it take God to create everything that is physical?
3. What process did God use to create?
4. Retell the six days of creation. Show how Day 4 goes with Day 1; Day 5 with Day 2; and Day 6 with Day 3. What does this tell you about God?
5. According to the Bible, how is God different from the things He created?
6. What is the purpose of Day 7?

Part 2: Creation of Man—How One became Two and Two became One

On the sixth day of creation, God made a special creature—a human being. God used dust of the earth to make man's body, into which He breathed life. God called this human good. God named him Adam, which means "human," and God gave him a beautiful garden for his home. The One True God gave Adam authority over all created animals and also the job of naming all the creatures of the earth. All that God made was good.

Adam was lonely. God caused a deep sleep to fall on Adam; then God performed the first surgery in history. He took a rib from Adam and created a separate being--two different sexes. The female was called Eve, which means woman, because she came out of man. God brought her to Adam, who said, "This is now bone of my bones and flesh of my flesh." The man was united to his wife, and they became one flesh.

God created the man and his wife in a special way: in His own image. Since God is Spirit, His image was impressed upon them in ways that express God's person. God shaped their bodies with eyes, for God can see; with ears, for God can hear; with senses, for God can feel; with a mind and a brain, for God can think and has all knowledge. People are special, distinct from animals.

Like God, man has things we cannot see. Man has a will; he can decide things. He has a mind; he can know things. He has emotions; he can feel and understand things. Man has ethics; he knows deep inside his being that he should do right. Man has morals; he knows deep inside that God exists. God put His own knowledge in the earth. Man can learn by studying the plants, animals, land, and sea. Man can love, appreciate, plan, utilize, and artistically design things. God gave man the ability to have authority over the animals. Man should not abuse his authority over other men, or animals, nor set his will against God.

On the seventh day, God made a special day of rest for man, a day for man to reflect and remember his Creator God. On the other six days, man worked. In the evenings, God walked and talked with Adam and Eve in the perfect, beautiful garden.

Discussion: Part 2

1. Explain how one person became two and two becomes one. What does this tell you about the importance of commitment in marriage?
2. Did God design two men or two women to have a marriage union? Why or why not?
3. What does it mean that God created man "in His own image?"
4. If humans are created in God's image, how does that affect the value of each person? Are women more or less valuable than men?

Assignment

Choose at least one of the following. Write your answers and be prepared to share them with the class.

1. Many cultures have their own version of how the world came to be. Some are considered legends; others are more factual. Prepare a summary for the class explaining how the beginning of the world is viewed in your country.

2. Many places in the Bible make it clear that man is to worship the One True God, and only Him. In your observation of people here and in your home country, what are some things people substitute for God in their worship?

3. Read the account of creation in your Bible: Genesis 1-3. If possible, read in your heart language as well as English. Write any questions you have about these chapters.

4. Worship is a difficult concept to explain. What is your understanding of the word worship?

5. Many students have been taught that the world began with a Cosmic Bang and evolved from there. If you are interested in learning how some scientists reconcile the Biblical account of creation with the theory of evolution, visit www.creationscience.org or www.answersingenesis.org. These websites will give considerable insight into the conflict between creationism and evolution.

6. Create a collage of some of the most beautiful places you've ever visited. Print it and prepare to share it with the class.

Paintings by Edward Hopper

Nighthawks

A Room in New York.

Chapter 3: Relationships and Ruin
Where did conflict come from?

Nighthawks

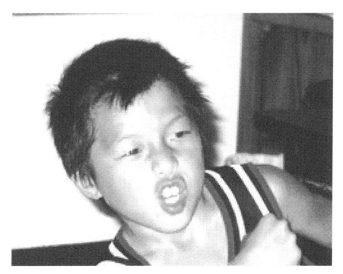

Conversation: Relationships

1. What are some characteristics of any positive relationship, whether marriage, friendship, work or play?
2. Why are friendships so important in our lives?
3. What can ruin relationships?
4. Could you continue being friends with someone who hurts you, either physically or verbally?
5. How do you act with someone who disagrees with you?

Social situations: Developing friendships

Internationals have observed that Americans in general tend to be friendly, but it's difficult to develop strong, deep friendships with them. Common interests are an important component of friendships. Building on these interests takes time, patience, effort, and observation.

1. Think of a person whom you might like as a friend. What characteristics of that person interest you? List them.

2. How might you arrange to spend more time with this person?

3. There are some unwritten social rules that might be useful in developing this friendship.

   a. Personal space—Observe how closely people stand when they're talking. Is this similar to or different from your culture?

   b. Eye contact—Although it may be uncomfortable for you, try to establish direct eye contact when talking with or listening to someone. Eye contact in this culture communicates interest and understanding. Looking down or around communicates boredom or disagreement. This doesn't mean you have to stare at the person's face, but when you're talking or listening, look frequently at the other person.

   Practice this and see how others respond.

Pronunciation

Past tense verbs

Past tense verbs that end in a voiced consonant other than d, or in a vowel sound, are pronounced with a strong d ending. The e of the final ed is silent.
Practice these verbs yourself, then with a partner. Look for other past tense verbs that fit this pattern and add them to your notebook.

observe	observed	live	lived
arrange	arranged	disguise	disguised
stare	stared	reply	replied
kneel	kneeled	lie	lied
follow	followed	open	opened
deceive	deceived	sew	sewed
call	called	try	tried

Pronunciation problems

Small differences in English sounds are difficult for language learners to distinguish and pronounce. Listen as the teacher says each word pair; then repeat each word. Then get with a partner. While one says a word from each pair, the other marks it with a pencil. After you've checked your work, switch roles and do it again.

th/f

a. thin fin   c. thirst first   e. thick flick   g. throw foe

b. thread Fred   d. throne phone   f. three free   h. thank frank

List some of the English sounds that cause you trouble. Work with your teacher or a partner to read the words with that sound. Then practice pronouncing them correctly.

Perception: Idioms, phrasals, culture clues

Idioms and phrasals are problematic features of English speech, especially since they are so frequently used. While you may know the literal meaning of each word, the combinations are confusing. Listen to the following dialogue and underline any idioms or phrases that are unfamiliar to you.

Stan: How's your class project coming? The presentation is due next Friday, right?

Joe: It's coming along great! Ever since Maria started meeting with me, we've made a lot of progress. **Two heads are better than one**, you know.

Stan: Hmmm. Maria. Sounds interesting! Is she cute?

Joe: As a matter of fact she is. But you've got this all wrong. We've been **best buds** since junior high school. Since we're both at the same university, we've been **keeping track of each other**.

Stan. Are you sure you're just friends?

Joe: Yeah. Really! A couple of weeks ago, Maria had car trouble. She called me and I went over to check out her car. It just needed more oil. Hey, **a friend in need is a friend indeed**. We try to look out for each other.

Stan: So you're really sure you're not **in a relationship**?

Joe: I'm sure. Why? Are you interested? Maria and her boyfriend broke up last semester. They tried to **patch things up**, but it didn't work. Maybe I can arrange a **blind date** for you.

New expressions: Idioms and Phrasals

What do you think these might mean? How can you use them in your own conversations?

a. Two heads are better than one.
b. best buds
c. Keep track of each other.
d. just friends
e. A friend in need is a friend indeed.
f. in a relationship

g. patch things up

h. broke up

i. blind date

Collocations:

Collocations are word combinations that flow together naturally in English. They are predictable to the native speaker but not to the language learner. Correct collocation usage will help result in clear, precise communication.

    a. Make friends with
    b. User friendly
    c. Printer friendly
    d. Going out with/going with (in context of a relationship)
    e. Work it out
    f. Talk it out

Culture Clues: Individualism

Some observers say that America is an "I" culture; that is, a person's self interests are more important than group or family interests. This manifests itself in many ways, including how one chooses a college, a spouse, a career, or a place to live. It also affects friendships, work relationships, and marriages.

    a. Discuss the following:
        1) What is your opinion about our country's dating system?
           Is it a good way to prepare for marriage? Why or why not?
        2) Contrast or compare this with your home culture.
        3) In your country, what are the parents' roles in major life decisions?

    b. Over the years newspapers have carried personal advice columns in which a reader asks how to deal with some relationship issue. TV programs have brought two arguing people before a judge who asks questions and makes determinations. With a partner, write out a scenario for an "Ask Ann" advice column or a "Judge Judy" program. In it describe the conflict between two people; try to present both sides of the problem; then come to a conclusion. Be prepared to share your advice with the class. Possible ideas: credit card debt, unfaithful spouse, co-worker conflict.

c. What concerns do you have about your present (or future) relationships in America? At school? At work? In your social life?

d. Look at the following paintings and discuss the relationships depicted in them.

American Gothic by Grant Wood

Breakfast Table by Norman Rockwell

 Listening and Bible Knowledge

Listening: Reductions

Native English speakers usually do not pronounce every sound in a word, or even every word distinctly. Train your ear to listen for the content rather than the individual word or sound. If you want to sound like a native English speaker, practice these reductions and intentionally employ them in your conversations this week. These should not be used in formal speech or formal presentations.

a. **should have**—becomes *shudda*
   1) You should have gone to the picnic.
   2) I should have studied harder for that exam.
   3) They should have made less noise last night.
   4) Create other sentences using should have. Then practice using the reduced form.

b. **would have**—becomes *wudda*
   1) He would have made a good politician.
   2) We would have won the game if we had more strong players.
   3) She would have had an accident if she had not swerved from that car.
   4) Create your own sentences using would have. Then practice the reduced form.

c. **could have**—becomes *cudda*

   1) We could have had a birthday party for her.
   2) There could have been a lot more damage from that storm.
   3) Who could have guessed that the President would have come here?
   4) Create additional sentences using could have.
      Then practice the reduced form

d. **let me**—becomes *lemme*

   1) Please let me have a piece of cake.
   2) Let me help you!
   3) Why didn't he let me attend his game?
   4) Create other sentences using let me.
      Then practice the reduced form.

 Bible Knowledge

Part I: The Deceiver

According to the Bible, God is perfect and He made all creation perfect. The things we can see are physical; what we cannot see is spiritual. God created angels—spirit beings that man cannot see unless God makes them visible to man. Angels were created to praise God and to be messengers to man on earth.

God created all angels "good, but they do not have authority over the world and are not to be worshipped. They are not God. They do not marry, as they are spiritual beings. However, one angel named Lucifer became proud and rebellious. He said, "I will be like God." Because Lucifer wanted to sit in the Creator God's place of authority and not obey God, God threw Lucifer out of heaven, along with other angels that followed Lucifer. He became known as "Satan," "the devil," and the enemy of God and of good. Satan's followers became known as "evil angels," "fallen angels," or "demons." They also try to deceive man and create trouble between man and God.

 **Discussion: Part 1**

1. Why did God create angels?
2. How are angels different from man?
3. What was the purpose of angels?
4. Who is more powerful—God or Satan?

Part 2: The Perfect Couple

When God created human persons, they were good. There was no sin, no evil, no unhappiness, no jealousy or envy or death. The man, the woman, and all living creatures lived together in perfect harmony in their special home, the Garden of Eden. Man ate fruits and green herbs and root crops. God sent dew on the ground to water the plants of the field.

Because woman came out of man, God initiated marriage for them, and told them to have children. Marriage between a man and a woman was God's design and plan. Family was a part of God's design on the earth. Man and woman were both naked and not ashamed.

God provided all that the man and woman needed to fully enjoy life. Man worked in God's garden and enjoyed the perfect weather and the perfect environment. God told man to eat from every tree in the garden except for one in the center —"the Tree of the Knowledge of Good and Evil." God did not want man to know evil. He told them that if they ate the forbidden fruit, they would die. Adam and his wife were the perfect couple in a perfect world. Everything was good.

 **Discussion: Part 2**

1. Where did God put man to live?
2. Describe the Garden of Eden.
3. What could man eat from the garden?
4. What one thing was man not to eat from the garden?

Part 3: The Relationship is Ruined

Satan wanted man to worship him, so he disguised himself by talking through the most beautiful creature of the earth—the serpent. Satan asked the woman, "Did God forbid you to eat from every tree in the garden? The woman replied, "We may eat the fruit of the trees of the garden. But God told us not to eat or to touch the fruit in the middle of the garden or we would die."

Satan lied, "You will not die! God is keeping a secret from you. He does not want you to be like Him. He does not want you to know good and evil. God knows that when you eat that fruit, your eyes will be opened. Your mind will be enlightened!"

The woman looked at the tree. The fruit was pleasant to her eyes. She desired the fruit from the Tree of Knowledge of Good and Evil because she wanted to become wise. She took the forbidden fruit and ate it. She also gave a bite to her husband and he ate. On that day, sin and rebellion against God entered humans. On that day, man and woman began to age and die.

After they ate, their eyes were opened. Suddenly they knew they were naked. They sewed fig leaves together and made coverings for themselves. Their disobedience and rebellion against God shamed and dishonored them; and that evening when they heard the sound of the Lord God walking in the garden, they tried to hide from the presence of God.

God called to them, "Adam, where are you?" Adam said, "I heard your voice and I was afraid and ashamed because I was naked. So I hid myself."

"Who told you that you were naked?" God asked Adam. "Did you eat from the tree that I told you not to eat from?" Adam complained, "The woman gave me the fruit and I ate it."

God turned to the woman and asked, "What have you done?" The woman said, "It's the serpent's fault! He deceived me and I ate."

God always judges sin and wrong-doing. God gave the punishment for sin. God disfigured the serpent and made it crawl on its belly and eat dust. God said, "The woman's offspring will crush your head and you will strike his heel."

To the woman God said, "I will increase your labor and pain in child-bearing, and your desire will be toward your husband, and he will rule over you." Adam called his wife's name Eve because she became the mother of all living.

To Adam, God said, "I will curse the ground with thorns and thistles so that your labor will be difficult and your work will produce sweat. Eventually you will die and return back to the dust from which you were created."

Because Adam and Eve chose to disobey God, sin entered into the world. They were no longer the perfect couple in a perfect world. Everything changed.

 **Discussion: Part 3**

1. Tell or act out the story.
2. Whom did Adam blame?
3. Whom did Eve blame?
4. Describe the results of sin for each one: 1) the serpent, 2) the woman, 3) Adam

Part 4: God's Perfect Solution

After Adam and Eve sinned, they were ashamed and afraid and knew their own weaknesses. They tried to cover their nakedness with the work of their own hands—their own weaving. Yet their leaves only covered their human nakedness and not their sin and the nakedness of their heart. God had a better plan for them.

God provided animal skins to clothe Adam and Eve. The animal skins required the death of an animal—blood shed. No animal had ever died before. The animal's death and blood was the provided substitute for Adam's and Eve's sin. The animal skins were symbols of the Sacrifice needed for the covering of man's sin—restoring a right relationship with God.

God sent Adam and Eve out of the garden because He did not want them to eat of the Tree of Life and live forever in their sin. The Tree of Life was a symbol that man was designed to live forever. Man would now die! His body would return to dust until his body was resurrected and rejoined with his soul and spirit.

Before God sent them out of the garden, God gave Adam and Eve a future promise with future hope of a future Deliverer. God said, "I will put hatred between you and the woman, between your offspring and hers; he will crush your head and you will strike his heel." This promise is found in Genesis 3:15. For centuries people would look forward to a Perfect Substitute—the seed of the woman—who would deliver people from their sins.

As we continue to study the Bible, we will learn the identity of that Perfect Substitute for man's sin.

   **Discussion: Part 4**

1. What caused the first death in creation?
2. Why did God send Adam and Eve from the garden?
3. What did God promise would happen in the future?

 **Assignment:**

Choose at least one of the following: Write your answers and be prepared to share them with the class.

1. Relationships are essential to humankind. Yet they can be ruined by sometimes small and apparently unimportant things. Ask several people what they think builds relationships and what destroys them. Summarize the results of your investigation in at least two paragraphs.

2. Describe your very best friend, explaining the characteristics that make your relation ship strong. Illustrate some of these character qualities by real experience in your lives.

3. Read the account of Adam and Eve in your Bible (Genesis 2:4-3:24). If possible, read it in your heart language as well as in English. Write any questions you might have.

4. Create a concept map showing the results of sin and rebellion against God.

5. Create a mime depicting Eve's encounter with Satan.

The Blizzard of 1888 in New York City

Hurricane Katrina in 2006.
Which do you think did the most damage?
Why do you have that opinion?

Chapter 4: Catastrophes
Why are there so many disasters?

Conversation: Natural and man-made disasters

1. Have you or an acquaintance ever experienced a natural disaster? Tell about it.
2. Name some unnatural (or man-made) disasters. Are these preventable?
3. If you were at home, work school, shopping, or traveling and a natural disaster struck, what would you do to protect yourself and those you love?

 Social Situations: Responding to a man-made disaster

If you are involved in or witness a vehicle accident, there are certain things you should do. They vary from state to state, but usually include the following:

1. Call the police—911
2 Remain at the scene until police arrives
3. Remove injured people from imminent danger if possible
4. Exchange license, insurance, and contact information.
5. Complete an accident report for police within a certain number of days
6. Repeat verbally what happened, draw a sketch or take pictures for the police.

Activity: With a classmate, invent an accident scene.
Then role play proper response to the accident.

1. Be aware of special roadside signs relating to natural disasters. They include such headings as "Hurricane Evacuation Route," "Snow Emergency Route," "Snow Emergency Parking," and "Flood Area." If you are in such an area during a natural disaster, follow the signs and obey law enforcement officers.

2. Many communities have warning sirens for natural disasters. Find out if yours does, what the siren sounds like, and what action to take if you hear it.
3. It's wise to be prepared for various types of weather emergencies. Discuss the following and complete the chart, listing essentials you would need for each situation and procedures you should follow if you are faced with any of the emergencies listed.

Emergency Preparations

Type	Place	Provisions (I need)	Procedures (I should)
Snowstorm	Car		
	House		
Hurricane	Car		
	House		
Tornado	Car		
	House		
Wildfire	Car		
	House		

 ## Pronunciation

Past tense verbs
Those that end in a voiceless consonant other than t are pronounced with a strong t sound at the end. Practice these verbs yourself, then with a partner.

witness	witnessed
face	faced
distinguish	distinguished
mark	marked
practice	practiced
watch	watched

Pronunciation problems
Small differences in English sounds are difficult to distinguish and pronounce. Listen as the teacher says each word. Now get with a partner. While one says a word from each pair, the other points. After you've checked your work, switch roles and do it again.

a. fan van   d. fast
b. fail vale   e. leaf
c. feel veal   f. ferry very   i. fact vase

List some of the English sounds that cause you trouble. Work with your teacher or a partner to read the words with that sound. Then practice pronouncing them correctly.

Voice inflection

When a danger suddenly arises, you may need to warn others. Listen to your teacher say each of these phrases. Then take turns saying them with strong emotion.

•	••	•••
Stop!	I'm hurt!	Be careful!
Fire!	Watch out!	It's burning!
Help!	A crash!	Take cover!

Perception: Idioms, phrasals, culture clues

Listen to the following dialogue and underline any idioms or phrases that are unfamiliar to you.

Karen: Look at this! **It's raining cats and dogs!** When is it ever going to stop?

Annette: I don't know. The weather service has issued a flash flood warning for low-lying areas. So I guess we'll be **cooped up** in this apartment for at least another day.

Karen: I don't know about you, but I'm starting to get **cabin feve**r. This prolonged, heavy rain only happens **once in a blue moon** around here, but it had to come while you're visiting. I'm so sorry! I hope it doesn't' spoil your vacation.

Annette: Oh, this rain is just one of a series of unfortunate events. I felt **under the weather** when I left home. Then I almost missed my plane. Then the airline lost my luggage. They were swamped with complaints, so it took a couple of hours to finally get my bags. I've heard the expression, **"When it rains it pours."** So the flood warning doesn't surprise me a bit.

Karen: Well, let's **make the best of the situation**. Want to watch a DVD?

Annette: Sure. Why not? Do you have "The Perfect Storm?"

New expressions: Idioms and Phrasals

What do you think these might mean?
How can you use them in your own conversations?

a. It's raining cats and dogs.	b. cabin fever

c. once in a blue moon
d. swamped
e. when it rains it pours
f. Make the best of the situation.
g. cooped up
h. He felt under the weather.

If you do a computer search of weather idioms, you may find many others.   Look over the list and bring your questions to class next time.

Collocations and phrasal verbs

A collocation is a common expression formed by a relationship between two words that go together. Collocations are similar to phrasal verbs, but are not necessarily verbs. Read the lists below and discuss the meanings

a. Collocations
   1) frostbite
   2) snowdrift
   3) wind chill
   4) snowbirds
   5) snow job

b. Phrasal verbs
   1) rained out
   2) snowed in
   3) snowed under
   4) drowned out
   5) washed up

Culture Clues: Control over environment

Many Americans are concerned about the global environment. They like to control their "own private space" as much as possible, but sometimes feel helpless in regard to global environmental issues. Air and water pollution, greenhouse gases, solid wastes, global warming and depleting fossil fuels are topics of discussion, debate and political speeches.

Sit with a few classmates and discuss the following:

a. What have you noticed about the environmental habits of your neighbors here?

b. Do you think your country is more successful or less successful than the US in addressing environmental issues, such as recycling, emissions controls, use of plastics, water consumption, and lowering fuel consumption? In what ways?

c. How would you encourage others to be better stewards of the environment? Are there any changes you need to make personally in your environmental habits?

d. Some people who suffer depression are diagnosed with SAD: Seasonal Affective Disorder, which happens in areas of little sunshine for long periods (like the Pacific Northwest of the USA). Do you think you are influenced by the weather? How?

e. If you have time, see if your group can name five songs about the weather? Can you sing them? You might enjoy a computer search of this topic.

Listening and Bible Knowledge

Listening: Reductions

a. **did you** becomes *didja*
   1) What did you do after class?
   2) How did you manage to get an A on that exam?
   3) Where did you live before you moved into this apartment complex?
   4) Write your own sentence using did you; then read it as a reduction.

b. **want to** becomes *wanna*;
   wants to becomes *wanzta*
   1) I want to become a cancer research scientist.
   2) Fred wants to visit every continent during his lifetime.
   3) They want to win the swimming competition.
   4) Write your own sentences using want to and wants to; then read aloud.

Bible Knowledge

**Part 1: A Great Dilemma,
            Human Evil and God's Plan**

When Adam's descendent, Noah, was born, the earth was corrupt and filled with violence and warfare. As the population of mankind multiplied on the earth, rape and murder become more and more prevalent. The culture declined as humans chose a lifestyle of great sin. Wickedness became great on the earth and every intention of the thoughts of man was only evil continually. God is holy, so the LORD-God became sorry that He had made man. God's justice is right, and His judgments are pure. God knew that He had to punish man.

The only breath of fresh air was Noah, to whom God gave His grace. Noah found grace in the eyes of the LORD, for Noah was a just and righteous man. He was a man who had faith in God and walked in close fellowship with God. Noah had a wife and three sons—Shem, Ham, and Japheth.

God shared His plan with Noah. God told Noah to make a wooden ark—a boat—of special cypress wood. God gave very specific instructions, and Noah followed them exactly. Then God said, "I will cover the earth with a great flood that will destroy every living thing that breathes. Everything on earth will die. But I will confirm my covenant with you." So Noah, his wife, and his three sons and their wives entered the ark. They obeyed God's command to take into the ark a pair of every kind of animal and bird, even the small animals that scurried along the earth—male and female.   Noah also had to store food for his family and all the animals for a whole year.

Discussion: Part 1

1. If you had never before seen rain or water coming out of the mountains, would you believe God that there would be a flood?
2. If you were a young woman, would you have wanted to marry Shem, Ham, or Japheth? Why or why not?
3. Does God care about animal conservation? Does He want species to become extinct? What do you think?

Part 2: The Flood and God's Deliverance

Noah did everything exactly as God commanded him. Noah took seven pairs of animals—male and female—approved for eating and for sacrifice. He also took seven pairs of birds—in order that they would survive after the flood. When Noah was 600 years old, he and his family entered the ark. After all the animals were inside, God closed the door; they could not get out. They waited. . .and they waited.

Suddenly, after seven long days, the underground waters erupted from the earth and the rain fell in great torrents from the sky for 40 days and 40 nights—non-stop! The flood waters got deeper and covered the ground. The water lifted the boat from the earth. What a strange feeling that must have been for Noah and his family! As the water rose higher and higher, the ark floated safely on the surface. Finally the water covered the highest mountains. All living things on the earth died—all the animals and all the people were destroyed. The only ones who survived were Noah, his family, and the animals inside the ark. It was truly an Ark of Safety—a place of deliverance! The flood waters covered the earth for 150 days.

God remembered Noah and all the animals in the ark. God sent a wind across the earth as the floodwaters receded. The underground waters stopped flowing and the rains stopped. After five months, the boat rested on the top of Mount Ararat. But Noah still could not go outside. The waters continued to go down, and gradually other mountain peaks became visible. After another 40 days, Noah opened the window and released a dove. The dove returned, for the waters were not yet dried up off the earth. Seven days later, the dove went out and returned with an olive leaf in her mouth. Trees were starting to grow! After seven more days, the dove did not return to Noah.

The waters were dried up. Noah looked outside and continued waiting until the surface of the earth was completely dry. Then God told Noah to disembark from the ark, along with all living things. What a sight that must have been!

Immediately, Noah built an altar to the LORD and offered burnt offerings of every clean animal and every clean bird. The offerings were a sweet aroma to the LORD and a sign of Noah's faith and obedience.

Discussion: Part 2

1. Retell the story of the flood. Compare the biblical account with your culture's flood story.
2. What important way did Noah thank God for delivering him?
3. Why did Noah take seven pairs of some animals and one pair of others?

Part 3: God's Covenant with Noah

God promised Noah that He would never again flood the earth, even though man's imaginations in his inner self are evil from his birth. God promised that while the earth remained, there would be seedtime and harvest, cold and heat, winter and summer, day and night.

God blessed Noah and his sons and told them, "Fill the earth!" He also told Noah that animals would now fear man and man fear animals. Before the flood, man did not eat the flesh of animals, but from now on, everything moving thing that lived and moved would be food for man. However, man was not to eat the blood, for life is in the blood.

After the time of the flood, God established a law that if one man killed another, his life was to be taken. This law for human government was to protect man, who was created in God's image.

God established His covenant with Noah and his sons. God's covenant was—"Never again will there be a flood that will destroy all people on the earth." God gave the rainbow as a symbol of his covenant with man.

Discussion: Part 3

1. What could be eaten? What was forbidden?
2. Compare man's relationship with animals before and after the flood. What was different?
3. Why did God make a law allowing taking the life of a killer? Is that a valid reason, in your opinion?
4. Has God kept His covenant with mankind? What is the evidence?

Assignment:

Choose at least one of the following. Write your answers and be prepared to share them with the class.

1. Society in Noah's time was in a rapid downward spiral. People did whatever they wanted with little regard for God or others. Do you see any parallels with today's world? What happens when self displaces God or others as our focus?

2. After a serious flood of the Red River in Minnesota in 1997, children wrote poems about their experience. Here is one:

    "A Poem that Makes 'Sense'" by Ashley

    > A flood is gray.
    > It sounds like rushing water.
    > It tastes like swamp water.
    > It smells like dead fish.
    > It looks like a war zone.
    > It makes you feel like crying.

    (www.fema.gov/kids/pm_manvel.htm)

    Have you had an experience with a severe flood? What were your thoughts and feelings? Express them either in writing or drawing.

3. Read the account of the Flood in your Bible: Genesis 6-9. Write any questions you might have.

4. Draw or paint illustrations of different parts of this story. Consider Noah's preparation for the Flood, loading the ark, the flood itself, the conclusion, God's symbol of his Covenant, Noah's worship.

5. Over 200 ancient flood traditions exist globally from every populated continent. All these traditions include the following: 1) universal destruction by water, 2) a boat, 3) a small group of people saved. Many also include some aspect of man's evil and wickedness as the cause. Does your home culture have such a tradition? If so, recount it here.

Paintings by Frederic Remington

Pony War Dance

Pony Express

Chapter 5: United Nations?
How did the various cultures begin?

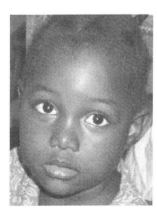

Conversation: Culture

1. You have now lived in at least two countries. In addition to language, what major cultural differences did you first notice when you came here?
2. What cultural differences have been the most difficult for you?
3. There are many different aspects of culture: language, traditions, values, holidays food, religions, dress. In your opinion, what are the most distinctive aspects of your country's culture?
4. Collin Raye wrote the lyrics to a song about differences. In part, they say:
    "I laugh, I love, I hope, I try.
    I hurt, I need, I fear, I cry.
    And I know you do the same things, too.
    We're really not that different, me and you."
        From "Not that Different" by Collin Raye

Do you think people from different backgrounds are more similar or more different? In what ways?

 ## Social Situations: Weddings

Because this country is comprised of people from many ethnic and religious backgrounds, there probably isn't such a thing as a "typical American wedding." However, if you are invited to a wedding, there are some components common to most situations.

1. **Attire (what to wear):** Business formal is usually safe—a suit and tie for a man, a dress or dressy outfit for a woman. Usually a wedding is one of the most formal events in this country. However, some weddings take place at a beach, on horseback, on a boat, or other less traditional settings. In those cases, the invitation will usually specify expected attire.

2. **Gift (what to bring):** A gift is commonly welcomed and may be brought to the ceremony or reception. Many couples construct an online wedding registry of things they would like or need for their new home. Money is always welcomed, too.

3. **Ceremony (what to expect):** The actual wedding ceremony differs greatly according to the couple's religious beliefs—or lack of them. A Christian/church ceremony usually includes a procession of the bride and her attendants, who meet the groom and his attendants at the front of the chapel (sanctuary, auditorium). They exchange rings, listen to a message from the officiating pastor or priest, repeat vows of their marriage covenant, and kiss one another.

They are then pronounced husband and wife and walk happily down the aisle to greet family, friends and well-wishers.

A civil ceremony is often conducted in a courthouse, a home, or wherever the couple chooses. A judge or justice of the peace presides.

4. **Reception (the celebration party):** Attendance at the reception is usually by invitation only. If your invitation states something like, "Reception immediately following at…." If there is an RSVP card included, the bride and groom are counting the number attending. Because wedding receptions can be very expensive, some couples limit the number of guests in accordance with what they can afford.

Receptions can vary from wedding cake and punch to finger foods to a catered meal. There may or may not be dancing, alcoholic drinks, and a program.

This week, make an effort to learn more about wedding customs here.
There is probably a wedding channel on cable TV!

Pronunciation: Improving your speech

Syllable stress

In English, syllable stress is very important to understanding a speaker. The stress can totally change the meaning of a word (ex. content, content). Practice saying these words with correct syllable stress. What patterns do you notice?

procla**ma**tion	**thought**fulness	patri**o**tic
enunci**a**tion	**sleep**iness	syste**mat**ic
communi**ca**tion	**rest**lessness	proble**mat**ic
reco**gni**tion	**sel**fishness	me**chan**ic
per**cep**tion	**sin**fulness	e**lec**tric

hy**ster**ical	arche**o**logy	elec**tric**ity
hi**stor**ical	chron**o**logy	authen**tic**ity
eco**nom**ical	myth**o**logy	elas**tic**ity
e**lec**trical	the**o**logy	a**gil**ity

Minimal pairs: l and r

Listen as your teacher says each word pair; then repeat each word. Now choose a partner. While one says a word from each pair, the other marks it with pencil. After you've checked your work, erase your marks, switch roles, and do it again.

a. lug	rug	e. alive	arrive	i. hail	hair
b. link	rink	f. belly	berry	j. steel	steer
c. lap	rap	g. pilot	pirate	k. file	fire
d. list	wrist	h. tally	tarry	l. heal	hear

Pronunciation practice:

l

location
homeland
building
invisible
Babel
babbling
rebellion
families
eventually
culture

r

reconciliation
racial
radical
computer
Persia
arrival
restaurant
westerly
shirt
department

Perception: Idioms, phrasals, culture clues

Idioms. Listen to the dialog below and underline any unfamiliar terms.

Wife: Honey, are you busy right now? I'd like to **have a word with you** about Amy.

Husband: Ok. What's the matter? You seem really upset.

Wife: I am. Maybe if I **talk this over** with you, I'll calm down. Amy's supposed to be my best friend, but lately, when I talk to her, it's like **talking to a brick wall**. I don't **get anywhere** with her.

Husband: What's this all about?

Wife: Have you seen Amy and Bill together lately? They're engaged, right? They're planning their wedding. But when it comes to financial planning, Amy is **speaking out of both sides of her mouth.**

Husband: What do you mean?

Wife: Well, she has all these dreams about a fancy house and beautiful furnishings and all, but she's also thinking about quitting her job! You know what she says? **Two can live as cheaply as one**." So she's not going to work!

Husband: Has she **talked this through** with Bill?

Wife: Not exactly. When he **brings up** the subject, Amy just goes on and on about this dream house. Bill **can't get a word in edgewise**.

Husband: Well, Amy always **speaks highly of you**. Have you tried to discuss this with her? Not **talk around the subject**, but really talk about it? Finances are one of the main issues in many divorces.

Wife: I don't want to offend her, but maybe I should be more direct and not **mince my words**. This is important. Ok. I'll confront her.

Husband: **Now you're talking**!

New expressions: Idiom and Phrasals

What do you think these might mean? How can you use them in your own conversations?

Idioms:
a. have a word with you
b. talk this over
c. talking to a brick wall
d. speaking out of both sides of her mouth
e. Two can live as cheaply as one.
f. talked this through
g. can't get a word in edgewise
h. speaks highly
i. talk around the subject
j. mince my words
k. now you're talking

Phrasals and collocations:
Discover the meanings of these phrases; then try using them in your conversations when appropriate.

a. talk back to
b. talk down to
c. talk _____ into_____
d. talk around the subject
e. talk trash
f. talk shop

Culture clues: directness, openness, bluntness, informality

a. Bill Perry, in *A Look Inside America*, (page 21) writes:
"The frontier made everyone—settlers, pioneers, and later cowboys—equal in position and rank. All of them started with the same kind of unsettled land. Life was simple but hard. Thus informality became a normal pattern of behavior."
Sit with a partner and discuss the following pictures in relationship to these culture traits. What would life have been like in such a setting? How would people interact?

"Lumber Camp" by Frederic Remington

b. Is your home culture more formal or less formal than America's? In what ways?

c. You have probably observed Americans in everyday situations, such as work, classes, shopping, commuting. Make a list of behaviors (manners) or speech habits that you feel are formal. Then list the informal manners. Which do you prefer? Why?
(example: "Yes, sir" is formal.   "Yeah, sure" is informal)

Listening and Bible Knowledge

Listening: Reductions

Who did you, who did he, and who did she are often reduced to whoja, whodee, whoodshee. Practice these reductions yourself, then with a partner.

Who did you ask to your party?
  (Whoja ask to your party?)
Who did he go biking with yesterday?
  (Whodee go biking with yesterday?)
Who did she go shopping with?
  (Whodshee go shopping with?)

Who did you work with on your project?
  (Whoja work with on your project?)
Who did he choose as his VP?
  (Whodee choose as his VP?)
Who did she learn to cook from?
  (Whoodshee learn to cook from?)

Bible Knowledge

Part 1: The Beginning of Languages

After the Great Flood, many people were born to Noah's three sons. God's design was for these three major people groups to live together within boundaries that God defined, and to scatter over the whole earth inside their own boundaries.

At that time all the people of the earth spoke the same language and used the same words. The people became one large culture that began moving east together. They settled in a large plain named Shinar and began building a large city with bricks and tar (pitch). They planned to build a city with a tower that reached into the sky. They wanted to become famous. They did not want to scatter over the whole earth as God instructed them to do. Once again man refused to obey God and chose to go their own way.

The Visible Image of the Invisible God came down to look at the city and the tower. He saw that they were trying to make an important name for themselves and had forgotten about worshipping the One True God. The people worshipped a 'mother-son' deity (like Ishtar and Tammuz) and many other gods.

"Look," said the Visible Image to the Invisible God, "The people are united and they all speak the same language. Man is becoming so great that whatever they set their minds and will to do, they will be able to do it. Nothing will be impossible for them to do!"

Then God said, "Come let us go down and confuse the people with different languages so that they will not be able to understand one another." When that happened, the people stopped building the city. The people named the city 'Babel' because that is where the LORD confused the people with different languages. In that way, the One True God scattered the people over all the earth.

Shem moved east toward the mountains. Ham moved south, while one of his grandsons named Nimrod rebelled against God and became known as the greatest hunter-warrior in the world. Nimrod built many large cities and established cultures that lived in the Middle East. Japheth's families moved north and toward the sea.

From these ancestors' lines of descent and from these clans came all the nations of the earth. Each had his own land territory and his own family of languages.

Discussion: Part 1

1. What was the major danger of the people speaking the same language?
2. How did one world culture develop when man continued living in one large city group?
3. Who is the One True God? What is meant when God said, "Let us…?" Discuss the Visible Image of the Invisible God—Elohim God—the One God expressed as 'diversity in unity.'
4. At least how many different 'families' of languages were started during the time of the Tower of Babel—at the time of the confusion of languages.

Assignment

Choose at least one of the following. Write your answers and be prepared to share them with the class.
1. Directness and bluntness are often heard in communication. People say things like "That isn't right;" "I don't like that," and other very straightforward expressions. Is this offensive to you? In what ways do you need to adjust to this manner of speaking?
2. With a partner, write a brief script depicting two Americans disagreeing about some thing. Then write the same scenario as it would happen in your home cultures.
3. Do an internet search of songs of the American West. Look for the lyrics to such songs as "The Streets of Lorado," "Red River Valley," "Bury Me Not on the Lone Prairie" on YouTube.com.
   What do these songs tell you about the life of a cowboy or pioneer?
4. Read the account of the Tower of Babel in your Bible in Genesis 11.
   Write any questions you might have.
5. Do you think it is important for children to understand, appreciate, and participate in their first culture language and customs? How might you encourage that to happen?
6. List several things you wish Americans would understand about your first culture. Why are they important to you?

Going and Coming

by Norman Rockwell

Gas Station by Edward Hopper

Chapter 6: A Mobile World
Why are so many people relocating?

Conversation: Travel

1. Brainstorm for two with a partner and list as many different ways of travel as you can.
2. What is your most favorite method of travel? Your least favorite? Why?
3. Describe one of your most pleasant travel experiences.
4. Describe a trip that was memorable because of travel troubles.
5. What is the difference between emigrate and immigrate?
    Between immigrant and refugee?

Social Situations: Travel Etiquette

Perhaps you have wondered about appropriate manners in travel situations in this country. Think of behavior:

>   on public transportation
>   in an elevator
>   on an escalator
>   as a pedestrian (on a sidewalk, crossing a street)
>   in a car

1. What have you noticed in these places that surprises you?
2. What are the rules governing behavior in these public places?
3. Would you suggest different rules? What and why?
4. Have you ever observed "the ugly American" in your country? What was offensive?

Pronunciation: Improving your speech

Phrase stress

> In English, not only is syllable stress important, but so is phrasal stress. Phrases, which are groups of words within a sentence, have their own stress patterns. You may hardly even hear some words in phrases, while others are stressed.

   a. Content words are usually stressed. These include nouns, action verbs, modifiers, question words (who, what, where, when, why, how), and demonstratives (this, that, these, those) when they make the intent of the speaker clear.

   b. Function words are usually unstressed. These include prepositions, articles, conjunctions, and pronouns (usually). Sometime such words are barely spoken, but are still part of the sentence.

c. Practice saying these phrases aloud, applying the above guidelines

How are you?	What's the matter?
vote of confidence	take a cruise
make a difference	groups of words
catch the train	tired but happy
pack your bag	print your itinerary
hit the sack	call me later

Pronunciation problems

Review these words orally with your teacher. Then practice with a partner.

cl	**cr**
climate	create
classical	creative
clean	chronology
cleanliness	chronological
cleanse	chronic
clarify	crosswalk
classic	credit
classical	criminal
classification	cream

Perception: Idioms, phrasals, culture clues

Idioms in context: Listen to the dialog below and underline any unfamiliar terms.

Son: Dad, I really appreciate being able to go with you on this work project. That tornado was so devastating! There's so much rebuilding to do for the victims!

Dad: I'm glad it's working out this way, too. My two colleagues and their wives invited me to carpool with them, but I **felt like a fifth wheel.** I'd much rather go with you.

Son: Have we finished packing all the tools? It's really late and I'm tired. I think I'm **running on fumes** right now. And we've got to **hit the road** very early tomorrow.

Dad: I'm sorry what did you say? I lost my **train of thought.** I was thinking about those poor people who lost their homes. Tools? I guess I've been **asleep at the wheel.** Let's finish loading the pickup and **hit the sack**, ok?

Son: Yeah. Dad, do you think we'll really be able to **make a difference**? We're just two guys, and there are so many needs!

Dad: Don't forget, we're going to be part of a large disaster relief team. We don't have to **reinvent the wheel**. We just have to do the work we're assigned. You're a good hard worker. So am I. So, **where the rubber meets the road,** we will be a real help. I'm sure of it.

Son: Thanks for the **vote of confidence**, Dad. Now let's **grab a bite to eat** and **catch some z's**.

New expressions: Idioms

What do you think these might mean? How can you use them in your own conversations?

    a. felt like a fifth wheel
    b. running on fumes
    c. hit the road
    d. lost my train of thought
    e. asleep at the wheel
    f. hit the sack
    g. make a difference
    h. reinvent the wheel
    i. where the rubber meets the road
    j. catch some z's

Phrasals and collocations: Discuss the meanings of these phrases; then try using them In your conversations when appropriate.

crash	landing	**cream**	puff
	helmet		cheese
	course		pitcher
	barrier		sauce
train	of thought	**wheel**	of fortune
	an employee		fifth wheel
	gravy train		spin your wheels
			squeaky wheel
move	on	**fly**	by night
	over		swatter
	up		on the fly
	out		off the handle
	it		high flying

Chapter 6

Culture clues: Technology on the move

Advances in technology have made travel for business or pleasure much more convenient. However, the exponential increase in mobile phones, laptops, and other devices has created some culture clashes.

Sit with a classmate and discuss the following:

a. What common courtesies should you practice regarding cell phone use in these places?
   1) While driving
   2) In a class or meeting
   3) In the company of others (at work, a party, a meal, a car)
   4) On public transportation
   5) In public places (bank, store, restaurant, library)
   6) In a church or other place of worship

b. What courtesies should you practice regarding laptop use in these places?
   1) In a classroom
   2) On an airplane
   3) At a café

c. This week, be aware of your own technology manners, and mentally note those who are offensive in their tech etiquette. Plan to share your observations in our next class

 ## Listening and Bible Knowledge

Listening: Reductions

Need to and **needs to** are commonly reduced to *needa* or *neeta* and *needsta*. Try reading these sentences using the reduced forms.

I need a doctor.
  (I needa doctor.)
He needs to finish his project.
  (He needsta finish his project.)

We need to make reservations soon.
  (We neeta make reservations soon.)
She needs to speak more clearly.
  (She needsta speak more clearly.)

Bible Knowledge

Part 1: Travel to foreign lands

The worldwide flood and the confusion of languages did not permanently solve the problem of evil in the world. Sin continued and nations became very wicked, ignoring God's ways and turning to idols.

Ten generations after the flood, Noah's descendent had a son named Abram. God said to Abram, "Leave your country and your relatives and go to a land that I will show you. I will make you into a great nation. I will bless you and I will bless all other nations through your seed" (offspring).

Because Abram had faith in the One True God, he left his country when he was 75 years old, with his wife Sarai and his nephew Lot, and traveled to the land of Canaan.. While Abram camped at Shechem, the Visible Image of the Invisible God appeared to Abram and said, "I will give this land to your descendents." Abram built an altar and worshipped God.

Slowly Abram traveled south. During a famine he went to Egypt. When the famine ended, he traveled north. Again Abram worshipped the LORD.

After some family crises and a run-in with the wicked king of Sidon, Abram was afraid and discouraged. The Visible Image of the Invisible God spoke to Abram in a vision. God said, "Do not be afraid, for I will protect you. I am your shield, and your reward will be great." God further promised the land of Canaan to Abram's descendents.

Even though Abram had faith that God would protect him, he began to doubt God's promise because Abram and Sarai had no son. God told Abram to count the stars in the sky if he could. God promised that Abram would have as many descendents as the innumerable stars. Abram believed God, and God credited righteousness to Abram because of his faith.

 **Discussion: Part 1**

1. To whom do you go when you are afraid or discouraged? How are you helped?
2. Have you ever doubted a friend, family member or God when they made a promise to you? What happened?
3. How many stars have scientists counted? Have they discovered all the stars yet?
4. Who are the descendents of Abram? How many are they?
5. What made Abram righteous? What is righteousness?

Part 2: God's Covenant with Abraham

Abram was like you and me—he wanted to be certain of God's promise and asked God how He would give Abram a son. Why does man doubt the Supreme Creator of all things? Man desires a personal relationship with the Creator, but Satan tries to bring doubts and fears into man's human thinking.

In the covenant-making process, God told Abram to offer some animal sacrifices. Through that event, God gave Abram a vision that his descendents would become slaves in a foreign land for four hundred years before they could inherit the land God promised to them. God promised to keep His covenant through a blood-sacrifice provided by God Himself.

Although Abram had faith that God would provide the permanent Deliverer through his own son's descendents, Sarai was too old to have children. Rather than believe God, Sarai offered her Egyptian servant girl, Hagar, to Abram to carry his child. Ishmael was born when Abram was eighty-six years old. Though God promised to bless Ishmael, He intended to confirm His everlasting covenant through Sarai's own son.

God changed Abram's name to Abraham and Sarai's name to Sarah as He also changed Sarah's character. When Abraham was one hundred years old, Isaac was born to Sarah. God kept His promise and gave them a son who would be part of the lineage of God's promised Deliverer.

On several other occasions, the One True God spoke to Abraham and reminded him of the covenant. After Abraham's son, Isaac, was born, God challenged Abraham's faith and he obeyed God. Isaac grew to manhood, married Rebecca, and became the father of twins named Esau and Jacob

Before Isaac died, he verbally blessed his children. Jacob cheated Esau out of the best blessing by pretending that he was Esau. When angry Esau stalked Jacob and schemed to kill him, Rebecca sent Jacob to her brother Laban's place.

During his first night of flight, Jacob had a dream from God. He saw angels going up and down a stairway to heaven. At the top of the stairway was the Visible Image of the Invisible God, who said, "I am the LORD, the God of your father Abraham, and the God of your father Isaac. I am giving this land to you for your descendents' inheritance, and your descendents will be as numerous as the dust of the earth. They will spread over all the earth, and all the families of the earth will be blessed through you and your descendents." Jacob named the place Bethel which means "house of God," for there Jacob desired the LORD as his own God.

 **Discussion: Part 2**

1. When did God give the first promise of a Deliverer for man's sin?
2. What did God promise He would use to keep His covenant?
3. If there was blood shed to provide a covering for Adam's sin, do you think there will be blood shed when God provides a Permanent Deliverer for sin? What is God's pattern?
4. In what ways did God keep His promise to Abraham after Abraham's death?
5. What was God's promise to Jacob? How did this relate to His promise to Abraham?

 Assignment

Choose at least one of the following. Write your answers and be prepared to share them with the class.

1. Study the painting by Norman Rockwell. What do you suppose each child is thinking? Predict the outcome of this meeting. Have you ever experienced anything like this?

2. The listening section is taken from many chapters in the book of *Genesis*. If you want to read them in more detail, read *Genesis*. Write any questions you might have about the passages.

3. Covenants are found in the Bible in the lives of people who lived many years ago. Yet covenants are also used today. Research different types of convents used today. How are they similar to and different from God's covenants with Abraham, Isaac, and Jacob?

4. Are there promises, rules, items passed down from one generation to another in your family or your country? Describe their importance and explain their significance to you.

5. Abraham and his descendents lived in many different places and became cross-cultural communicators. You could assist people traveling to your home country by familiarizing them with manners and customs that are important there. Compile a mini-guide book that gives information on such things as visiting a home, time, public behavior, addressing elders, and other things you think would be useful.

6. Do a computer search of one of these subjects and be prepared to share your findings with the class:
    a. Advice to Americans traveling abroad
    b. Proper business attire and etiquette
    c. Business meeting etiquette

George Washington

Thomas Jefferson

Abraham Lincoln

Chapter 7: Leadership
Who needs leaders?

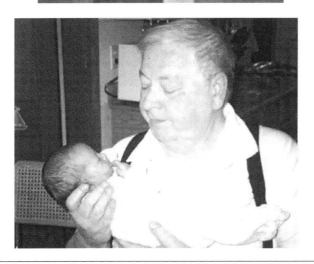

Conversations: Leadership

1. Do you think people are born leaders, or is leadership developed? Give examples.
2. What qualities make a good leader?
3. Describe different leadership styles. Here are some possibilities:
    charismatic, situational, participative, quiet, servant
4. What type of leader would you most likely follow? What type would you like to be?
5. Do you think it is important for a leader to be accountable to someone (be required to answer to someone)? Why or why not?

Social Situations: Behavior in meetings

Many jobs involve periodic "team meetings," whether in an office, production facility, service industry, or even class.

1. Role play that you are attending a company team meeting. You walk into the meeting and behave as you've observed others, or as you think others conduct themselves.

Then discuss with your group how to make the meeting more efficient and productive. List components of the meeting that need to be addressed, such as leadership, order, use of technology, who talks when, interest level, agenda, and other factors.

2. Research tips for effective meetings and report your findings to the class.

3. Compare and contrast team meetings in your home country with similar meetings here. What are the major similarities? Differences?

Pronunciation:

Minimal pairs: Practice these with a partner, taking turns reading. If you need more practice words, use a dictionary. You might also increase your vocabulary!

fl	fr
flee	free
flay	fray
flow	frozen
flew	fruit
fly	fry
flight	fright
flame	frame

Collocations:

(have no more…)	(from the…)	(no longer in…)
out of breath	**out of the** pool	**out of** date
money	blue	style
ideas	ordinary	sync
steam		touch
		action

lead the field	**follow** up
the way	through
the life of Riley	the pack
by example	in his footsteps

Perception: Idioms, phrasals, culture clues

Idioms in context: Listen to the dialog below and underline any unfamiliar terms.

David: Have you noticed a change in atmosphere in this office? It seems as though people are becoming too casual and careless around here.

Susan: Yes. I agree. In my opinion, "casual Friday" have become casual every day; and people seem to take their work less seriously. Did we **lead them astray** by instituting dress-down days?

David: Maybe it's time for a "Dress for Success" presentation. I really do believe our attire reflects our attitude. If we want professional results, we should appear professional to others.

Susan: David, you excel at **leading by example.** You represent the company and yourself well by the way you look. Why don't you plan a meeting to discuss this issue? You don't have to **lead everyone by the nose**, but you can set a higher standard.

David: Okay! But, Susan, you definitely **lead the field** here in proper business attire. Let's **close ranks** and maybe the **rank and file** will follow suit and dress up rather than down.

Susan: So are we going to have a meeting or just send a memo?

David: A meeting would probably be more effective. Then individuals would have to **break ranks** with the policy rather than privately disagree. Let's plan a meeting, then **follow through** with a memo. Maybe everyone will **get on board** and change the atmosphere around this office.

Susan: It's a **dog-eat-dog world** out there, so we need to create a competitive edge. Appearance does make a difference!

New expressions: Idioms

What do you think these might mean? How can you use them in your own conversations?

lead them astray	follow suit
lead by example	follow through
lead everyone by the nose	It's a dog-eat-dog world
lead the field	break ranks
close ranks	rank and file

Culture clues: Business attire

In groups or pairs, discuss the following.
Compare and contrast with attire policies in your home country.

1. Although many companies have initiated "casual Fridays" or "dress down days," others feel that professional appearance is always the safe route to success.
   What is the policy where you work?
   What is considered always appropriate attire for men? For women?
2. Do you think universities should consider a student dress code?
   Why or why not?
3. If you were to compose a dress code, what would it say? Why would you choose these guidelines?

Listening and Bible Knowledge

Listening: Reductions

Phrases using quantity words are often reduced. *A lot of* becomes *alodda*; *lots of* becomes *lotsa*; *a can of* becomes *acanna*; *a cup of* becomes *acuppa*. Practice these reductions yourself, then with a partner.

A lot of students are worried about finances.
(*Alodda* students are worried about finances.)
There's *lots of* snow in Chicago this week.
(There's *lotsa* snow in Chicago this week.)

He bought *a can of* soup.
(He bought *acanna* soup.)
Would you like *a cup of* tea?
(Would you like *accuppa* tea?)

Bible Knowledge

Part 1: Jacob's Descendents in Egypt

Eventually Jacob had 12 sons who grew up in the land of Canaan. Joseph, next to youngest, was a special favorite of his father. His jealous brothers sold him as a slave, so Joseph traveled with Midianite traders into Egypt. The LORD was with Joseph in numerous circumstances of life until Joseph landed a position as second to Pharaoh. During the time Joseph was in Egypt, Egypt became the most powerful nation in the world. Under Joseph's leadership, Egypt's crops prospered and the nation became even more wealthy.

During a famine in Canaan, Joseph's brothers journeyed into Egypt to buy food. They bowed before the powerful Joseph, who recognized his brothers but did not reveal his identity to them. Joseph wanted to keep his younger brother Benjamin with him in Egypt, but Judah, Jacob's fourth son, said to Joseph, "I cannot go back to my father without the boy. I guaranteed that I would be responsible for Benjamin, and that I would bear the blame forever if he did not return. So, please, allow me to remain here as a slave so Benjamin can be returned to his father, for I could never bare the anguish this would cause my father."

Joseph then revealed himself to his brothers and found a place for his father and his brothers to live during the famine. Joseph chose the region of Goshen for their flocks and herds. After elderly Jacob died, Joseph's brothers feared that Joseph might seek revenge on them, but Joseph wept and spoke kindly to his brothers. "Do not be afraid of me. Am I God that I can punish you? You planned evil against me, but God wove that wrong into good; and I will continue to care for your children."

 **Discussion: Part 1**

1. What does Joseph's reaction to his brothers tell you about his temperament? What are some things that might have made him kind-hearted, despite the treatment of his brothers?
2. How had God used Joseph's slavery to benefit the descendents of Abraham, Isaac, and Jacob?
3. Have you ever had an experience that seemed very negative but turned out to be positive? Tell the class about it.

Part 2: Moses becomes God's leader

Joseph lived to be 110 years old. Before he died, he reminded his brothers of God's promise to then: "God will surely come to help you and to lead you out of this land of Egypt. God will bring you back to the land of Canaan, for God promised that land to Abraham and to Isaac and to Jacob. When God leads you out, promise me that you will take my bones with you." The Egyptians embalmed Joseph after he died and placed his body in a coffin in Egypt.

The entire descendents of Jacob multiplied so greatly in Egypt that they became extremely powerful and filled the land. Eventually a new king came to power in Egypt who knew nothing about Joseph or what he had done. This king (pharaoh) made the Israelites slaves and forced them into hard labor. The Israelites built the supply cities of Pithom and Rameses. The ruthless Egyptian masters made their lives bitter and showed them no mercy.

The king of Egypt became fearful of the Israelites and ordered that every boy baby born to the Israelites must be killed.   The infant son of Amram and Jochebed was hidden by his parents for three months, but they knew they could not continue to conceal him as he grew and developed. They asked God for wisdom, and He gave them a plan to save Moses. The king's daughter found the baby, named him Moses, and gave him back to his own mother to nurse and care for until he was older.

Moses' mother nursed him and taught him about the One True God—the Supreme Ruler and Creator of all things. She probably told him about his heritage—about Abraham, Isaac, and Jacob, and God's promises to them. When Moses was older (perhaps school age), his mother brought him back to Pharaoh's daughter, who adopted him as her own son. Then she took him to live in the palace, and raised him as a well-educated Egyptian. (You can read about this in Exodus 2.)

Moses was then schooled in all the philosophies of the Egyptian and Eastern world. He may have read Sumerian documents and Indian mystical stories. Perhaps his mother's earlier teaching kept him interested in the Hebrew people, for when he grew up, he visited his own people and saw how hard they were forced to work.

Moses was shocked to see an Egyptian beating one of his fellow Hebrews. Moses' mother surely taught him about humans created in the image of God, so the sight of one man beating another sickened and angered him. When Moses thought no one was watching, he killed the Egyptian and hid his body in the sand.

The next day, when Moses visited his people again, he saw two Hebrew men fighting. "Why are you beating up your friend?" Moses asked. The man replied, "Who appointed you to be our prince and judge? Will you kill me as you killed that Egyptian yesterday?"

Moses was afraid that everyone knew what he did! Pharaoh heard what happened and tried to kill Moses. So Moses fled and hid in the land of Midian. It was there that God spoke to him and called Moses to become the leader of the Israelites.

 **Discussion: Part 2**

1. Compare Egyptian 'no-son' policy in this story to present-day nations. Who gives children to couples? Who protects babies?

2. Apparently, adoption was possible in Egypt, even adopting a child not from your own culture. What are some descriptions of adoption in your culture? Do people adopt from outside the family? Why or why not?

3. What are things Moses' mother taught him while he was still young? How do you think the mother got to be the person who nursed him? Was this happenstance? Luck? God?

4. Why do you think Moses was more concerned about the Hebrews? Can you see a place in the story where Moses' cultural identity 'crosses over' from Egyptian to Hebrew.

Part 3: Moses as the new leader

Years passed—40 years total—and the king of Egypt died. The Israelites groaned under the heavy burden of slavery and cried out for help—and their cry rose up to God. God heard their groaning, and He remembered his covenant promise to Abraham, Isaac, and Jacob. He knew it was time to act. The Visible Image of the Invisible God appeared to Moses in the form of a burning bush that was not consumed in the wilderness near Mount Sinai.

"This is amazing!" Moses said. "Why isn't the bush burning up?" God called to Moses from the middle of the bush, "Moses! Moses!" "Here I am," Moses said. "Take off your sandals; this place is holy ground. I am the God of your fathers—the God of Abraham, the God of Isaac, and the God of Jacob." When Moses heard this, he covered his face, because he was afraid to look at God.

The Lord-God said, "I see the oppression of my people in Egypt. I hear their cries of distress because of harsh officials. I am aware of their suffering. I came down to rescue them from the Egyptians and to lead them out of Egypt into their own fertile and spacious land, a land flowing with milk and honey. I will give the land to you. Go! Go to Pharaoh and lead my people out of Egypt!"

Moses argued with God that he was not capable of being such a leader. However, God persuaded him and promised to be with him and help him. God promised that all the people who wanted Moses dead had died, so Moses took his wife and sons and carried his staff and went back to Egypt.

Discussion: Part 3

1. When people are suppressed, to whom should they cry for help?
    Who is higher than any official or government?
    Who gave human government to people? For what purpose?
    When human government becomes corrupt and oppressive, what actions should godly people take?

2. It seems that Moses recognized the name—'God of Abraham, God of Isaac, and God of Jacob', for that is when he covered his face. Where do you think Moses first heard about this One True God?

3. How important do you think it is for parents to teach children about God?
    At what ages should parents teach these truths?
    How old was Moses when he first heard of God?
    Do you know of any quotes about teaching children while they are young?

Part 4: Moses leads and God provides

At age 80, Moses became the new leader of the Israelites, and the people began worshipping the One True God. Moses and his brother Aaron presented their proposal to Pharaoh. "The LORD God of the Hebrews wants us to take a three day journey into the wilderness to offer sacrifices to the LORD our God. Let my people go so that they may worship God."

Pharaoh replied, "Who is the LORD? I do not know your God and I will not let Israel go!" Pharaoh accused Moses of distracting the people and ordered the foreman to force the people to get their own straw for making bricks without decreasing their quota. The people groaned over this added burden and complained to Moses. Moses cried to the Lord, "Why did you send me? Pharaoh is now more brutal to your people."

Sometimes things have to get worse before they get better. God hardened Pharaoh's heart so that He could show Himself great and powerful in the land of Egypt. The people worshipped many gods, including the Nile River, frogs, gnats, flies, and the sun. Because wicked Pharaoh did not allow the Israelites to sacrifice to the One True God, the eternal, self-existent God struck the Egyptians with ten plagues that targeted the many gods of Egypt. The river turned to blood. Frogs and gnats and swarms of flies created chaos. Other disasters occurred, but still Pharaoh would not let the Israelites go to worship the One True God.

Finally God told Moses to announce to Pharaoh: "At midnight, the LORD will pass through Egypt and the Death Angel will kill every firstborn and the people will mourn and wail." To the Israelites, Moses gave God's message: "Kill a perfect lamb, drain the blood, and apply the blood to both sides and the top of the doorposts of each house. Get ready to leave Egypt. When I send the Death Angel and I see the blood, I will pass over your home and not harm the firstborn."

Things happened just as God had said. During the night Pharaoh finally cried to Moses, "Get out! Leave Egypt! Take your flocks and herds with you!" Pharaoh's officials and the Egyptian people respected Moses because they considered him a very great man, so the Egyptians looked favorably on the people of Israel. When the Israelites asked for silver and gold and fine clothing, their Egyptian neighbors gave them gifts so that they would not leave Egypt empty-handed. Six hundred thousand men plus women and children left Egypt, just as God had promised. Each year since, the people of Israel celebrate the Passover Feast to remind themselves of God's substitute provision for them…a firstborn animal died so the firstborn son could live. Moses continued leading the people of Israel for forty years until a new generation was ready to enter God's Promised Land.

 **Discussion: Part 4**

1. What Substitution-Sacrifice was needed to purchase back the firstborn son? Why?
2. What major way did the whole nation respond to the LORD'S Deliverance?
3. How do you think the Israelites felt as they gathered their belongings and left Egypt?

 Assignment

Choose at least one of the following. Write your answers and be prepared to share them with the class.

1. Research the Jewish customs associated with Passover celebrations today.

2. Read the account of the Passover and the exodus in the Bible. It is found in Exodus 12 Write any questions you have.

3. Prepare a skit depicting the last night of the Israelites in Egypt.

4. Have you ever experienced a time when you were asked to do something you felt very unqualified to do? Describe the situation and your response to it.

5. Many other adventures occurred as the people left Egypt. If you are not familiar with the story of the Red Sea crossing, read about it in the Bible (Exodus 14).

6. Read the Song of Deliverance in Exodus 15: 1-21.
   Sing it too! Make up your own tune.
   Better yet, make up a 'song of Deliverance' if you also have experienced special deliverance by God. Research songs about Moses, and share your findings.

7. When Moses faced difficult challenges, he seemed to respond in two ways First he protested to God. Then he acted obediently. How do you respond to challenges in your life?

The Problems We All Live With
by Norman Rockwell

Abraham Lincoln
by T.H. Benton

Chapter 8: Justice
Is there such a thing?

Conversations: Laws and justice

Justice seems to be elusive. All around the world, justice and injustice create tensions, riots, and even wars. Divide into groups and discuss the following quotations.
Do you agree or disagree with them? Why?

1. "Justice and power must be brought together, so that whatever is just may be powerful, and whatever is powerful may be just." --Blaise Pascal

2. . "Justice denied anywhere diminishes justice everywhere." --Martin Luther King Jr.

 ## Social Situations: Controversial topics

In some cultures discussion of politics, religion, and social issues is not only acceptable, but expected. In other cultures, however, these topics require careful consideration, lest you damage or destroy relationships.

1. Anna Post suggests these guidelines (taken from www.huffingtonpost.com, 2/21/08)
    a. "Just the facts." Stick to facts and avoid opinions.
    b. "Have an exit strategy." Plan ahead how to escape the conversation if it becomes heated. Consider these phrases:
        1) "For me, it's private."
        2) "I'll have to consider that."
        3) "I guess we don't see eye to eye."
    c. "What's your position?" Why are you having this conversation? To persuade? To explain?
    d. "Know when to fold 'em." Some situations are unsuitable for potentially confrontational conversations. Weddings and holidays are times for making happy memories, not making enemies."
    e. "Assume nothing." You do NOT know how the other person feels.

2. Listen to others in conversation and notice how they handle controversial issues. Be prepared to share your observations.

 ## Pronunciation:

Minimal pairs:

bl	br
blanch	branch
bleed	breed
blew	brew
bland	brand
bloom	broom
bleach	breach

Intonation: Tag questions

Tag questions are question phrases placed at the end of declarative sentences, thus turning the sentence into a question. They are often confusing because the voice intonation is the key to understanding whether it's a true question or a fact waiting to be confirmed.

If it's a genuine question (the answer is unknown), the voice will rise at the end.
If it's a confirmation question (fact to be confirmed), the voice will fall at the end.

Practice these sentences using both rising and falling inflection.

   a. The policeman stopped you for speeding, didn't he?
   b. You're going to court today, aren't you?
   c. That judge has a reputation for fairness, doesn't she?
   d. You're planning to plead guilty, aren't you?
   e. The friend was found innocent, wasn't she?
   f. The jury didn't deliberate long, did they?

Perception: Idioms, phrasals, culture clues

Idioms in context: Listen to the dialog below and underline any unfamiliar terms.

Pete: Have you noticed the crime rate is actually down in our neighborhood this month? Previously when teens committed a crime, they either **got off scott-free** or **just got a slap on the wrist.** Now that we have a new judge who goes **by the book**, things are changing.

Ed: Maybe some of the leaders who are used to **beating the rap** or **copping a plea** are now finding that real justice and truth will prevail. They can't continue posing as **a wolf in sheep's clothing** forever.

Pete: The new judge gives the perpetrators a **fair shake,** but if they break the law, they pay. It might not be **an eye for an eye or a tooth for a tooth**, but the consequences are real and proportional. Community service is one of the positive changes.

Ed: Community service and restitution to the victims are reasonable penalties. But what about **serving time**? Do you think justice is served if they don't go to jail?

Pete: In my opinion, jail time is needed for violent criminals. But these guys are not getting away with their crimes. Whether they're white, Hispanic, or African American, they need to keep the law. No one is exempt.

Ed: It's not like the **kangaroo courts** of the Wild West. The court in this neighborhood is maintaining justice for its citizens. It's a big improvement!

New Expressions : Idioms

scott-free
got a slap on the wrist
by the book
beating the rap
copping a plea

Posing as a wolf in sheep's clothing
a fair shake
an eye for an eye or a tooth for a tooth
serving time
kangaroo courts

Phrasal verbs:

keep the rules
a promise
an appointment
up with something

take an oath
the Fifth
the stand
on a lawyer or client

break the law
a promise
someone's heart
the news to someone
into a building or safe

go easy on
scott free
by the book
off on a tangent
along with something

Collocations: legal terms

in contempt of court
session
favor of

on the bench
trial
a technicality

under oath
appeal

hung jury
jury is out

off the record
for the record

get **off** lightly
given a fair shake

Culture clues:

Americans are known to value equality and fairness, to work diligently to develop and maintain human rights for all citizens. Yet even in this century, there are gaps in equality.

    a. From your reading and observations, list some areas of inequality that still exist.
    b. How does your country address similar issues?
    c. Do you think prejudice plays a part in inequality and injustice? Why or why not?

Listening and Bible Knowledge

Listening: Reductions

a. kind of becomes kina
   1) I'm kind of hungry right now.
   2) What kind of dog is that?
   3) He's kind of handsome, don't you think?
   4) That music is kind of loud for my taste.

b. sort of becomes sorda
   1) Susan seems sort of depressed today.
   2) Our new neighbor said he's sort of getting used to the weather here.
   3) What sort of job do you have?
   4) Jake is sort of short for a basketball player, but he's really good.

Bible Knowledge

Part 1: Israel in the Wilderness

During Israel's wilderness journey, the people faced many challenges. At one point, they came to an oasis, but the water was too bitter to drink. The people complained and turned against Moses, but the LORD provided good water for them. Later, they complained about lack of food and thought they would starve to death. Again the LORD provided all that they needed. God sent special bread, manna, each day and quail for meat. God gave specific instructions to gather only enough for one day, but some selfish people disobeyed and gathered too much. That food rotted and smelled horrible. God was not pleased with their disobedience and asked, "How long will these people refuse to obey my commands and instructions?" Yet still God met their needs.

As Moses led the people through the wilderness, they saw the awesome glory of the Visible Image of the Invisible God as a pillar of cloud by day and a pillar of fire by night. When the pillar moved, the people moved. When it stopped, they stopped. Thus the LORD guided them through the desolate land.

Moses and the people of Israel faced many hardships on their journey. Jethro, Moses' father-in-law, visited Moses in the wilderness and brought Moses' wife and two sons to him. Moses told Jethro about God's wonderful power and deliverance. "Praise the LORD!" Jethro said. "I know now that the LORD is greater than all other gods because he rescued His people from the oppression of the proud Egyptians." Jethro offered sacrifices to God and joined the elders of Israel in eating a sacrificial meal in God's presence.

Jethro saw that Moses was burdened by many problems. He counseled Moses to teach God's decrees to the people, to give them His instructions, and to show them how to conduct their lives. He advised Moses to select capable, honest men who feared God and hated bribes to help solve disputes among the people. These men brought the major problem cases to Moses for his decisions.

In this way God provided for the people the leadership and justice they needed.

 **Discussion: Part 1**

1. Describe God's provision for the community of Israel.
2. What were the people instructed by the LORD to do for food?
3. How did God image Himself for the children of Israel?
4. Jethro was not an Israelite but he confessed the Self-Existent God as the One True God. Is the One True God for only one nation?
5. How did Jethro describe the character of the Egyptians. How might this characteristic destroy a man? A nation?

Part 2: **The Law of the LORD**

God put His Law on the earth at Creation. Man's authority came from God's Rule, with man in subjection and obedience to the Supreme God. Sin brought rebellion and disobedience to God's Rule, although civilizations kept social laws that helped hold cultures together. Many codes existed at the time of Moses, but moral codes were horizontally related—man to fellow man.

When God established this new nation, Israel, he gave them His code that surpasses other horizontally-related moral codes in existence. God's Law Code came in written format, written by the hand of God. God created humans and he has exclusive claim on them. God's moral code is both vertically related to God and horizontally related to man.

God's Law gave commands for how to live in obedience to God, as well as commands on how to live in a cultural community without violating man's image made in the Visible Image of the Invisible God. God's Laws were moral commands. His Law has 10 codes—the Ten Words (or the Ten Commandments). This is what the LORD God said:

1. **Have no other gods except Me.** All other gods are man-made and are in conflict with the One Supreme God. This command is centered on the being of God. The issue is who will have the allegiance or loyalty of your worship. The consequence for failing in the command would be that the people would be rooted out of the land and scattered into all the nations.

2. **Do not make any images** fashioned like anything in the heavens or on the earth or in the sea. Do not bow down to them or worship them, for I AM the LORD your God....
This command is centered on the image of God—on the visible Image of the Invisible God. The issue is fidelity to what God has disclosed about Himself. Once people make images of God, generations following them will make images and will worship them instead of the One True God.

3. **Do not misuse the Name of the LORD your God**. Do not use God's Name over and over again in rituals for your own selfish purposes, or in a careless manner in conversation. This command is centered on the issue of fidelity to the Name, the Person, and the work of God. God would not leave anyone unpunished who disobeyed this command.

4. **Observe the Sabbath Rest Day by keeping that day separate from regular daily work.** God had given this day to worship the Lord and to teach children to worship only the One True God. The Sabbath Day (the 7th day) for Israel was their "Covenant Day," a day when one will not work for material gain in life but will think of the greater value of eternal things. It is also to be a day of rest.

5. **Honor your father and your mother**, that you may live a long full life on the earth. Just as you are to teach your children, so you are to honor those from the past who taught you. In the way that you show proper regard for your parents, you are showing regard for yourself and those who follow you.

6. **Do not murder.** Sanctity of life is to be valued because man was created in God's image. The consequence for disobedience is death—and that should be physical death meted out by human government, not by revenge.

7. **Do not commit adultery**. Sanctity of sex and marriage are rooted in God's creation of humans as one man and one woman that are to have lifetime commitment to each other. Desires are not to be the central focus of life.

8. **Do not steal**. Property rights, family rights, and community goods are to be valued. There is to be no fraud (no deception) in using measures, money, or in selling or using land. A person is also not to rob God. Man is not to exploit the poor or the widow.

9. **Do not testify falsely against your neighbor**. Truth is to be valued in the judiciary courts and in the marketplace, including the labeling of prices on goods that your neighbor buys. There is to be no bribery because bribes cause truth to break down

10. **Do not covet**. Coveting is internal. While the other commands were external, this one relates to the inner being of man, to the totality of the person. The mind, the reflective place, determines the choices. This is a summary command that includes all the other commands.

Coveting self-acclaim removes God as the center of one's being. Coveting sets up idols and images that replace God. Coveting power takes human credit for things done in God's Name. Coveting material things destroys the day of worship. Coveting to have all the honor steals the honor the parents deserve. Coveting to the extent of killing another person destroys life. Coveting another's mate destroys marriage. Coveting property, money, and fame destroys and robs others. Coveting the limelight removes truth as the light.

God's Law can be summarized in two commandments: "You should love the LORD your God with all your heart, with all your soul, with all your mind, and with all your strength; and you should love your neighbor as yourself."

These laws are perpetually (continually, unendingly, forever) binding to all generations. Do everything to preserve life and truth and God. Do everything to protect and value your fellow man, treating him as created in God's image.

Discussion: Part 2

1. List the issue involved in each of the commandments.
2. Relate the commandment on God's Name to prayer and rituals.
3. Relate the commandment on adultery to purity before marriage. How might pre-marital sex destroy the sanctity of sex and marriage?
4. How do these commandments relate to exploiting the poor, the widow, the orphan, or the foreigner? (Exodus 22:21-27 and 23:9-11)
5. Relate the commandment on false witness to the court system. How does "oppressing foreigners" relate to this commandment?

Assignment

1. Alexander Solzhenitsyn wrote:
    "Justice is conscience, not a personal conscience but the conscience of the whole of humanity. Those who clearly recognize the voice of their own conscience usually recognize also the voice of justice."
    Do you think it is possible for governments or societies to balance freedoms, rights, responsibilities, and justice? How?

2. Obtain a DVD or VHS copy of the movie, *The Ten Commandments*, starring Charlton Heston. Watch it and compare it with the biblical account. Write your questions or comments.

3. Research Moses' "Song of Deliverance," sung after the crossing of the Red Sea. Listen to George F. Handel's "Israel in Egypt" and write your reaction to it.

4. Human rights are often in the news. What countries would you say lead the world in providing human rights to all its citizens? What countries have the worst human rights records? How would you suggest they change?

5. Several books and movies address racial or other inequalities and injustices. Chose one of these and read/view it, preferably with a friend. Be prepared to share what you have learned.
    A Raisin in the Sun (DVD or book)   *Uncle Tom's Cabin (DVD or book)*
    To Kill a Mockingbird)DVD or book)   *The Untold Story of Emmett LouisTill (DVD)*
    Radio (DVD)   *Remember the Titans (DVD)*

6. Read the Bible account of God's lawgiving in Exodus 21 and 22. Write your questions and/or comments. Consider how well you have kept God's Laws.

7. Read the American Pledge of Allegiance. Do you think Americans are keeping their pledge? Why or why not?

8. God's whole being is bound up in His Person and His Name.
    Man's whole being is bound up in walking/keeping/observing God's Law/Commandments. How would you answer the following?

    a. Can a man truly say he is worshipping God when he is not paying his employees?
    b. Can a man truly say he is worshipping God when he is gossiping against his neighbor or co-worker?
    c. Relate man's worship with other areas of everyday life.

The Runaway by Norman Rockwell

Gulf Stream by Winslow Homer

Chapter 9: Worries, Fears, and Promises
What hopes and fears are common in all cultures?

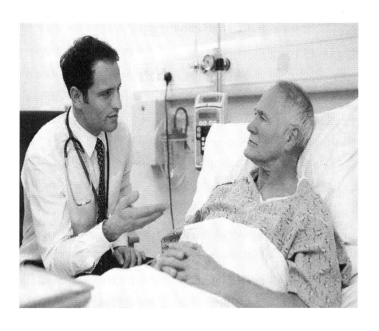

Conversations:

Hopes and fears are common experiences in every culture and at every level of society. Political turmoil, financial crises, family problems cause people to worry, lose sleep, and even become sick. Divide into groups or pairs and discuss the following:

1. What other kinds of things do people worry about?
2. How do you handle worry?
3. What happens if we let worry control us?
4. The ultimate worry is death. How can we overcome this worry?

Social Situations: Helping someone in a crisis

Whether with a co-worker, a classmate, a friend, or a family member, chances are that you will be in a situation in which someone you know faces a serious crisis. What can you do to help? Here are some suggestions. Discuss them with your classmates and teacher, and add other possibilities.

Do's	Don'ts
1. Listen—really listen	1. Assign blame
2. Reflect on the emotions being expressed	2. Try to shortcut the grieving process
3. Stay calm yourself	3. Act impulsively
4. Define the problem and consider choices	4. Ask too many questions
5. Guide the person into a plan of action	5. Make false promises
6. Network with others	6. Pressure the person to make false commitments
7. Provide hope—Biblical resources, community resources	7. Brush off emotions with clichés
8. Refer to a qualified counselor	8. Counsel beyond your abilities
9. Provide real, practical assistance like food, clothing, etc.	9. Ignore needs if you can help provide

Pronunciation

Minimal pairs:

gl	gr
glue	grew
glow	grow
gland	grand
glass	grass
glamour	grammar
glub	grub
glimpse	grimace

Intonation: Choice questions

Choice questions are questions with the word or, giving the hearer a choice between two or more options. They are often confusing because the speaker may hardly enunciate or, thus leaving the hearer unsure of the real intent of the question. Hearers may answer with a yes or no, rather than one of the choices.

The voice inflection will rise on the words indicating the choices, or the choice words will be stressed. Practice these sentences, using rising inflection or stronger stress on the choices.

- a. Do you want chocolate or vanilla ice-cream?
- b. Is his jacket black or brown?
- c. Will Susan bake the cake or buy it?
- d. Is Kiko a graduate student or undergraduate?
- e. Should we turn left or right at Chicago Avenue?
- f. Do you talk on the phone or in the phone?

Perception: Idioms, phrasals, culture clues

Idioms in context. Listen to the dialog below and underline any unfamiliar terms.

Jim: Did you hear the gossip around the water cooler? People are saying that next week the boss is **handing out pink slips** to 25% of the staff!

Pete: Are you serious? Who started that rumor? I heard he's hiring 25% more people! Somebody's got **to have their wires crossed**!

Jim: Well, maybe we can **hope for the best but prepare for the worst**.

Pete: Unless we get some official word, I'm not giving up hope. Jim, maybe you're just a big **worry wart**.

Jim: How can you say that? I'm just a realist. The economy is **in shambles**. Our sales are down. **I'm on pins and needles** wondering if I'll have a job next week. What are you **pinning your hopes on**, anyway?

Pete: Facts. Just the facts. I refuse **to get down in the dumps** over rumors. Sometimes people **make mountains out of mole hills**. Hey, here comes the boss. Why don't you just **straight-out** ask him?

Jim: Are you kidding? I have **butterflies in my stomach** every time I see him!

Pete: Well, don't give up hope. Our department had increased sales last quarter. And some people are being assigned to new territories. So maybe there's **light at the end of the tunnel**. Never fear! There's nothing to worry about. You know the old saying: "**It's not work that kills, but worry**." So, come on! **Look on the bright side!**

New expressions: Idioms

What do you think these might mean? How can you use them in your own conversations?

pink slips	down in the dumps
wires crossed	make mountains out of mole hills
worry wart	butterflies in my stomach
in shambles	there's light at the end of the tunnel
on pins and needles	look on the bright side
pinning your hopes on	

Collocations: hope, worry, fear

hope so	give up hope	worry over	with fear	deal with fear
hope not	live in hope	worry about	in fear of	get over fear
hope for	pin hopes on	for fear of	out of fear of	put fear into

Culture clues: "Doing" versus "Being" orientation

Over the years, because of the pioneering nature of America's development, people gradually moved from a "being" orientation to a "doing" orientation.

Bill Perry writes:
"People began to feel important and valuable more from their job (company manager, businessman, sales representative, etc.) than from their family relationships. It became more clear in the middle to late 1800's, between the Civil War and World War I. During this time American society went through its deepest change. Many people moved westward and bought unsettled land. This created national markets for goods and services. New technologies in transportation, communication and industry created larger companies and businesses. The growth of bigger companies required changes in banking, steel, oil and insurance companies. It also created the need for managers and bureaucrats, which strengthened the "doing" or work orientation, and made it a permanent part of North American culture."
(*A Look Inside America,* p. 19)

Find a partner or two and discuss the following questions.

  a. What evidence have you seen or heard of this "doing" focus?
  b. In your home country is success in one's job more important than success in one's *family*? Or is the *family* more important?
  c. As you talk with Americans, notice how often one's work is discussed. Is this common in your home country? If not, what is a prominent topic?
  d. What suggestions would you give for balancing "doing" and "being?"

Listening and Bible Knowledge

Listening

Past tense verbs: Be aware of these rules when you're listening.

   a. Those ending in D or T are pronounced with an extra syllable (id)
      1) He **waited** five hours for tickets to the concert.
      2) The boss **demanded** that his employees arrive at work on time.
      3) Have you ever **wanted** to travel to Alaska?
      4(The singer **decided** that he dedicated his song to the wrong person.

   b. Those ending in a vowel sound or voiced consonant other than D are pronounced with a strong D sound.
      1) Susan **seemed** delighted with your gift.
      2) Our neighbor **grabbed** his snow shovel and shoveled my driveway.
      3) Have you **hugged** your grandchildren lately?

   c. Those ending in a voiceless consonant other than T are pronounced with a T at the end.
      1) He **sipped** his tea slowly because it was very hot.
      2) Ed's father **smoked** a lot and coughed a lot.
      3) The cat **scratched** me when I touched him.

 ## Bible Knowledge

Part 1: Israel in the Promised Land

Finally, after forty years in the wilderness, the Israelites, also known as Jews, entered the promised land of Canaan. God had kept them safe, provided for them, and led them as He had promised.   Sadly, the people of Canaan rejected the One True God and fought against the Israelites. But God protected His people as they settled in the land promised to Abraham, Isaac, and Jacob.

The Lord ordained priests to oversee the animal sacrifices and to lead in worship as the Jews celebrated the various feasts and special holy days God had appointed. Each year they remembered God's Passover and sacrificed a lamb to signify their sorrow for sin and their faith in God's promises of forgiveness. Once a year, the high priest went behind a sacred veil which separated the people from the holy presence of God. There the priest represented the whole nation before God.

After many years, the Israelites crowned a king named David, whom God called "a man after my own heart." David wrote many songs which are recorded in the Book of Psalms. His son Solomon built a beautiful temple in which the Jews could worship. Non-Jews who believed in the One True God could also worship in the Court of the Nations.

God spoke to the people through godly men called prophets. Through these prophets, the Lord warned Israel when they sinned, that if they continued to sin, He would allow a foreign nation to overrun their country. In spite of these warnings, Israel was disobedient and rebelled against God. The people rejected His laws and killed some of the prophets who testified against them.

Finally, after eight hundred years of rebellion, Israel was taken out of her own land and made captive in the nations of Assyria and Babylon There the people of Israel, enslaved and far from home, experienced many emotional ups and downs. They feared God and their captors. They hoped to return to their land, but when given opportunity, some chose to stay. They knew the promises of God, but they also knew the messages of the prophets. The consequences of their sin and ignoring God's Law were very serious.

 **Discussion: Part 1**

1. Describe how God kept His promise to Abraham, Isaac, and Jacob.
2. What was the job of the high priest? Why did he offer sacrifices?
3. How was David known? How are you known by others?
4. What was the job of the prophets? What did Israel's disobedience cause?

Part 2: The Prophets' Messages of Hope

Despite Israel's rebellion, God continued to speak through prophets during the Jews' captivity. Some of the messages were calls to repentance, while others were prophecies about the Savior who would come to rescue sinful mankind. The One True God did not forget His promises to send a Deliverer.

The prophet Micah foretold the exact city where the Savior would be born and described His eternal nature, saying, "Out of Bethlehem shall the One come who will rule in Israel, whose existence is from old, from everlasting."

God even revealed that the coming Savior would descend from the royal line of king David.

Through the prophet Malachi, the Lord described a special messenger who would announce the coming Savior and prepare the people to receive Him.

Zechariah prophesied, "O daughter of Jerusalem: Behold, your King comes to you. He is righteous and has salvation; humble, and riding on the foal of a donkey."

King David described how the Savior Himself would know in advance that one of His close friends, whit whom He ate bread, would betray Him.

And Zechariah even recorded that the price of the betrayal would be thirty pieces of silver.

Through the prophet Isaiah, God foretold that the coming Savior would be tortured by whipping, and that His face would be spat upon.

David described the method of execution as "piercing the Savior's hands and feet, yet not breaking any of His bones," that the Savior would say, "My God, My God, Why have You forsaken Me?" and that onlookers would laugh and ridicule the Savior, saying, "He believed that the Lord would deliver him."

David also wrote that "The Savior's bones would be out of joint and in His thirst He would be given vinegar to drink," and that the Savior's persecutors would "divide His clothes among them, and gamble for His robe."

Isaiah said that onlookers would be astonished when they saw how the Savior's face was disfigured from the torture.

The prophecies in God's book even describe how one day, David's descendants, the inhabitants of Jerusalem, would "look at the Savior whom they had pierced."

All this…and more…was written in the Scriptures many hundreds of years before the Savior came. God made clear that He had not forgotten His promises. The Redeemer would come in God's appointed time.
(Taken from God's Story, p. 30-31. Used with permission)

 **Discussion: Part 2**

1. Where did the prophecy say the Deliverer would be born?
2. Who would be one of the Savior's ancestors?
3. Who would betray the Savior? How much would the betrayer be paid?
4. How did David describe the treatment of the Savior?
5. When were these prophecies written?

Assignment

1. The people of Israel both feared the future and hoped for deliverance. What are some of your hopes and fears? How might you address them?

2. Do you think we can place our hope in governments or world leaders? Why or why not? Write an essay or draw illustrations for your answers.

3. Obtain a DVD or script of *God's Story* (www.gods-story.org) Watch it and write your questions and/or comments. You may be able to obtain it in your first language.

4. Current economic situations have created fear in many people. Research an area of interest to you (job market, housing industry, small businesses, etc.) and prepare a report to share with the class. Include current trends, projections, and possible solutions to the situations. Use PowerPoint or other graphics to illustrate your findings.

5. The Bible offers hope for many of life's situations. Use a concordance to find verses on hope and write a summary of your findings.

6. Obtain a copy of *The Hope*, produced by Mars Hill. Watch it and write your reactions.

Christmas at Home by Grandma Moses

A Tramp on Christmas Day
by Grandma Moses

Chapter 10: Hope Arrives!
What is the best thing that has ever happened to you?

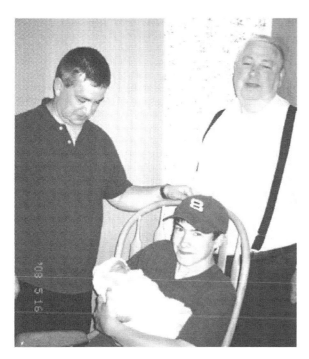

Conversations:

Someone once wrote, "Hope springs eternal in the human heart." Divide into pairs and discuss the following:
1. Would you say that you are a hopeful person? A pessimist? Why?
2. Have you ever felt helpless? Explain.
3. What is the main thing on which you base your hope for the future?
4. What role does a new baby play in a family's hopes?
5. Sometimes people purchase new things in hopes of being happy. Do you think a new house or new car can provide happiness? Why or why not?

Social Situations: Welcoming a new baby

When the first baby is born to a couple, it is common for friends or family to host a baby shower. Those who are invited bring gifts for the baby, and sometimes for the new mother. Many couples will create a baby gift registry at department stores. This is a list of items the parents want or need for their little one.

1. Discuss with the class how to use a gift registry.
2. What types of items are usually listed?
3. What is the typical program at a baby shower?
4. In your country, what are the customs associated with the birth of a baby?

Pronunciation

Short vowel sounds:

a	e	i	o	u
bat	bet	bit	bot	but
bag	beg	big	bog	bug
ham	hem	him	hom	hum
pat	pet	pit	pot	putt
mat	met	mitt	mot	mutt
gat	get	git	got	gut
mad	med	mid	mod	mud

Practice these short vowel sounds until you can distinguish each one. It will take much practice, but keep working on these difficult sounds.

Intonation: Phrase stress

In English, phrases within sentences are spoken as units. Content words, which convey the main meaning, are stressed, while function words like prepositions (of, to), articles (a, an, the), pronouns (I, you, me), and conjunctions (and, but, or) are not usually stressed.

Listen to the following sentences; then repeat them.
Practice saying them with correct phrasal stress.

1. Mary and Joseph lived in the town of Nazareth.
2. Tyler wanted to go to the race, but he didn't have a ride.
3. People in our neighborhood lock their doors at night.
4. Leo is very proud of his new sports car.
5. When the robber entered the store, a security camera took his picture.

Perception: Idioms, phrasals, culture clues

Idioms in context: Listen to the dialog below and underline any unfamiliar terms.

Lisa: Andy, we need to talk.

Andy: Not now, honey. I'm on the phone with an important client. In a minute.

   (A half hour passes. Andy comes into the living room, where Lisa is crying. Their new baby is asleep on her lap.)

Andy: What's wrong, honey? Why are you crying?

Lisa: You really don't know? Ever since you and Tom **gave birth to** this new company, you have no time for me—OR the baby! I was hoping we could spend a quiet evening together, just the three of us…you, me, and the baby….NOT you, Tom, and a client!

Andy: But, Lisa! Our company is **going great guns**. Sales are **off the charts**. We're so excited about this success, we're almost **bursting at the seams**!

Lisa: **Meanwhile, back at the ranch,** your wife is bursting into tears, and your baby doesn't even know who you are! Somehow, Andy, you've got to develop a balance between work and home. If not, I'm afraid **it's the end of the line** for us. I can't go on like this.

Andy: **Whoa**! You're talking serious stuff here! I'm not that **overboard** with work, am I?

Lisa: Think about it. When was the last time you and I just sat down and talked? Or took the baby for a stroller ride—together? I'm afraid **the almighty dollar** is your new love, instead of us.

105

Andy: But, Lisa! I just want you and the baby to have a nice home, a nice car, and beautiful things. And they cost money. What else can I do? I have to work hard!

Lisa: For one thing, you can leave your work at work. For another thing, I don't need all this stuff you're talking about. I'd rather have a small, cozy house with time for the three of us, than all the marble kitchens and SUV's in the world. What really is important to you? I read once, "**Where your treasure is, there will your heart be also.**" Where's your heart, Andy? **Make up your mind**!

Andy: Oh, Lisa! I've been so blind! What I thought was need has turned to greed, and I didn't even notice. I am so sorry!

Lisa: Andy, if I didn't love you, I'd have left long ago. You've been **selling your soul to the company store**. What does it profit a man if he gains the whole world, but loses his own soul? Nothing. Nothing but pain and empty dreams. Are you really willing to make some changes and make a commitment to all of us?

Andy: WOW! You're right! You and the baby deserve more—more attention, that is. I'll have to figure out how to **cut back** on work. I can't "**throw the baby out with the bath water**," but I sure can make some adjustments in my work schedule. **Don't get your hopes up too high**. This won't happen overnight. But it will happen. I promise. I'm going to work to earn your respect instead of more money.

New expressions: Idioms

What do you think these might mean? How can you use them in your own conversations?

going great guns   the almighty dollar
off the charts   make up your mind
bursting at the seams   selling your soul to the company store
Meanwhile back at the ranch "throw the baby out with the bath water"
It's the end of the line   Don't get your hopes up too high
Whoa!   overboard

"Where your treasure is, there will your heart be also."

Culture clues: Materialism

Comedian Jack Benny was well known for being a cheapskate. He did not like to part with his money. One of his skits went this way:

> Mugger: Don't make a move! This is a stickup! Now come on. Your money or your life!
> Jack Benny: (Silence)
> Mugger: Look, bud! I said, "Your money or your life!"
> Jack Benny: I'm thinking! I'm thinking!

Many Americans are accused of parting too easily with their money. Rather than saving for a rainy day, they have made the acquisition of material things and comforts their highest value. People are known by others for their beautiful houses, expensive cars, elegant clothing, and lavish lifestyles.

There is a huge contrast between the "have's" and "have not's" of society, even though we are all "created equal." This focus on things is even evident in schools, where children prize a certain brand of shoes or shirts, and where those who have make fun of those who have not. Thus, people are valued for what they own rather than for what kind of person they are.

Parents are divided on this issue. Some try diligently to help their children develop values that stress character rather than things. Others try desperately to "keep up with the Jones's," and find themselves deeply in debt. Holiday gift giving is often one source of conflict in this issue of meaning over matter.

 **Discussion:** Break into groups and discuss the following questions:

1. Think of some of the people in your circle of acquaintances. Without naming names, what evidences of materialism do you see?

2. How can you strike a balance between need and greed?

3. Think of some films you might have seen, or news articles, that depict materialism gone too far. How are values portrayed in these instances?

4. In your country, is materialism a big problem? In what ways is it evident? How might it be lessened?

Listening and Bible Knowledge

Listening: Body language

    a. Body language accounts for approximately half of what we communicate. While technically it isn't "listening," body language is an important component of communication. Someone has written, "Body language comes in clusters of signals and postures, depending on the internal emotions and mental states. Recognizing a whole cluster is thus far more reliable than trying to interpret individual elements." A partial list of message clusters includes:
        1. Aggressive body language
        2. Attentive body language
        3. Bored body language
        4. Greeting body language
        5. Ready body language

    b. Since greetings are part of most social interactions, we will consider just a few elements of greeting body language.

Handshakes may tell much about those who are greeting each other. The strength, temperature, and duration all send signals. A firm grip shows confidence, while a limp grip may indicate timidity. A hot or cold handshake may indicate fear or nervousness, while a long handshake can indicate pleasure and can signal dominance.

Waving is often done from a distance to acknowledge the presence of someone you know. "A big overhead wave can attract a person from some distance. This also makes others look at you and is not likely from a timid person. A stationary palm, held up and facing out, is far less obvious and may be flashed for a short period, particularly if the other person is looking at you."

Facial signals not only convey greetings, but reactions as well. Such expressions include smiling, frowning, raising the eyebrows, eye contact, and looking at the floor.

    c. Practice various greeting elements with your classmates and discuss your reactions to what is communicated to you by their body language. Then intentionally begin to incorporate some of these elements into your own interactions with others.

    d. Compare and contrast Western body language with that of your home culture.

*See http://changingminds.org/techniques/body/greeting.htm

Bible Knowledge

Part 1: The Promised One Arrives

One dark night, the One True God broke a long silence by sending the brightness of His glory into the world as the Light of the world in human flesh. The Invisible God placed the Creator-God of mankind into the womb of a virgin named Mary. Mary was not impregnated with God's seed. This birth was called the 'seed of woman' in Genesis 3:15. This was something done as a miracle by the Spirit of God.

The Visible Image of God, Jesus, left heaven to enter a human body as a man. The Invisible God assumed the title Father to Jesus, who assumed the title Son, a Son that could only be begotten by God and one that can never be replaced. This firstborn One and Only Son permanently housed in His physical body the fullness of divinity. God, who in the past spoke to man through His prophets, spoke to us in these last days by His Son, through whom God made the worlds.

God's angel Gabriel announced to Mary, "Rejoice, for God favors to bless you! Do not be afraid, for you will conceive a son who will be great and will be called the Son of the Highest. You shall call His name Jesus, and the LORD-God will give Him the throne of his ancestor David, and He shall reign forever and there will be no end of His kingdom."

Mary was confused for she was a virgin and had never had sexual relations with any man, but the angel confirmed that this birth would be from the power of the Highest God and that the son born would be called the "Son of God." Gabriel instructed Joseph to marry Mary to provide the proper cultural care for the virgin chosen to bear this special child. Both Mary and her fiancé, Joseph, were descendents of the family of David and could trace their genealogy back to Abraham and to Adam.

During the time of Mary's pregnancy, she visited her relative Elizabeth who was also pregnant. Filled with God's Spirit, Elizabeth cried out, "Blessed are you who believed and who was chosen among women and blessed is the fruit of your womb!" The baby inside Elizabeth leaped for joy when Mary entered the room, causing Elizabeth to call Mary's baby her LORD. Mary said, "My soul magnifies the LORD and my spirit rejoices in God my Savior, while I am His lowly handmaiden. Holy is His Name! He scatters the proud and puts down the mighty, while He exalts the lowly and fills those who are truly hungry… just as He spoke to our ancestor Abraham…"

Mary and Joseph lived in the northern town of Nazareth but they traveled south to the city of Bethlehem to register in their ancestral place to pay their taxes as decreed by Caesar Augustus. In those days, Palestine was under Roman rule. They searched for a private place for this special son's birth, but all the inns in Bethlehem were full. They found lodging at the outer edge of the city in a village called Ephrata which was still a part of Bethlehem.

So it was in 'Bethlehem-Ephrata' that Mary brought forth her firstborn son and wrapped him in strips of cloth and laid him in a manger—a food trough for sheep. Becoming human was a humbling experience for the Visible Image of the Invisible God. This child was Emmanuel (or Immanuel), which means, God with us.
(See John 1:1-18, Luke 1 to 2:1-7 and 3:23-38, Matthew 1, Colossians 2:9, Hebrews 1:1-2, Philippians)

 **Discussion: Part 1**

1. Describe the relationship of the Invisible God with His Visible Image (Jesus) while He lived on the earth.
2. What kind of woman birthed Jesus, the Visible Image of the Invisible God? Why was this important?
3. Christ's arrival is celebrated at Christmas around the world. How is the biblical account different from the traditions practiced in your country?
   How is it the same?

Part 2: Amazement of the Shepherds

The highest heavens adored God's Son on the night he was born. The Father pleasingly approved and verified the fullness of deity in His Son. God the Father sent hundreds of thousands of angels praising God who announced His Son's birth to shepherds watching flocks of sheep on the hillsides of Bethlehem-Ephrata, the homeland of former King David.

Shepherds in the 'Bethlehem-Ephrata' area raised Passover lambs for the Temple's annual atonement sacrifices. An angel of the LORD stood before the shepherds and the glory of the LORD shone all around them, and the angel said to them, "Do not be afraid, for I bear the greatest joyful news you ever heard and this news is for all people. Tonight Messiah the LORD is born in the city of David."

An angel told the shepherds to find their Messiah-Deliverer "wrapped in strips of cloth lying in a 'manger." The shepherds knew exactly where to go! Most likely, God's Son was born inside the shepherds' 'birthing cave' that was ceremonially clean and empty, as it was the grazing-season of the sheep.

A multitude of angels praised God saying, "Glory to God in the highest and on earth peace, goodwill toward men." When the shepherds arrived at the place where the Visible Image of the Invisible God was born as a human, they fell down on their faces and worshipped Him. Only God is to be worshipped! Truly this was the Son of God who became flesh and blood through a water-birth delivery, similar to the birth of every human being on the earth.

This is a great mystery that our finite minds will never completely comprehend, but the shepherds believed the saying and returned and glorified God for all the things they had heard and seen—just as the angels told it to them. After they saw the baby, they told everyone they met all that the angels told them about the child. Everyone marveled! But Mary kept all these things and pondered their meaning in her heart.
(See Luke 2:8-20)

 **Discussion: Part 2**

1. Which angel brought the message to Mary and to Joseph? Do we know the name of the angel who spoke to the shepherds? Is it important?
2. From what famous king did Mary and Joseph trace their ancestry?
    Do you remember what promises God made to this king?
3. What was so special about the Bethlehem-Ephrata area? What was the purpose of the Passover lambs? What do you think the connection might be between the lambs and the Promised One?
4. Whom did the shepherds worship? The angels, Mary, or God's Son?

Part 3: Prophecy that Messiah Came

When God's Son was physically eight days old at the time of His circumcision, Joseph and Mary took Him to the Temple in Jerusalem to present Him to the LORD, for Jesus was born under the covenant of Abraham. At this time, his physical parents named Him Jesus, the name that the angel mentioned before He was even conceived.

According to the Mosaic Law, the mother had to perform specific regulations concerning purification following the birth of a child. The parents offered a sacrifice of two young pigeons or a pair of turtledoves as was stated in the ceremonial Law.

During this time Simeon served in the Temple, and it had been revealed to him that he would not see death before he had seen the LORD'S Messiah. So the Spirit of God led Simeon into the temple on the day when the parents brought in the Child Jesus, to do for him according to the custom of the law.

Simeon was a just and devout man who longed for the Consolation of Israel, so as he took the child into his arms, he blessed God and said, "LORD, now you can let me die in peace for my eyes have seen Your Salvation which You have prepared before the face of all peoples, a Light to bring revelation to the Gentiles, and the glory of Your people Israel." Joseph and Mary marveled at those things which Simeon said about Jesus.

Then Simeon blessed the parents and said to Mary His mother, "Surely, this Child is destined for the fall and rising of many in Israel, and for a sign which shall be spoken against…Yea, a sword shall pierce through your own soul, and the thoughts of many hearts will be revealed."

Also in the Temple was eighty-four year old Anna, a prophetess, who after seven years marriage to her husband was a widow who devoted her life to serving God in the temple with prayers and fasting night and day. She entered the instant that Simeon blessed the child, and she also gave thanks to the LORD. Anna spoke of Him to all people who looked for redemption in Jerusalem.

What was supposed to be a normal day in the life of parents turned out to be an extraordinary day for Joseph and Mary as they were continually amazed at God's revelation about the Child to people who came near him! (See Luke 2:21-38)

 **Discussion: Part 3**

1. Jesus was born into one specific culture; and His parents devoutly followed what God had established for that culture. What does the fact that Mary and Joseph offered a sacrifice tell you about the parents and about the mother's need for purification?

2. The angels, shepherds, then Simeon and Anna all related their message to previous words from God regarding the prophesied Messiah/Redeemer/Deliverer who was to come. What is your favorite part and why?

Assignment

1. . Body language is important, but we have explored only a small portion of physical communication. Research other aspects of body language and present a summary to the class.

2. While Christmas is supposed to be a celebration of Christ's birth, it has become a major retail money-maker. Note some of the excesses you have observed regarding Christmas in this country. What is your opinion about the traditions and practices?

3. There is much more in the Bible about the birth of Christ. Read Matthew chapter 2 and summarize (1) the Wise Men from the East, (2) King Herod's terrible decree, (3) God's protection of His Son, (4) the family's life in Nazareth.

4. Business schools sometimes include body language strategies as part of their instruction on conducting successful business meetings. Research the importance of body language in business settings. Then prepare a skit or role-play that demonstrates how posture, conduct, and other physical factors affect business meetings.

5. If you have children (or may have children some day), what would you hope for them? How could you realize these hopes? What factors are beyond your control?

6. Research some common ways of celebrating Christmas in this country. Compare and contrast them with celebrations in your home country. Create a chart visualizing some of the components of Christmas celebrations.

Paintings by Norman Rockwell

Girl with a Black Eye

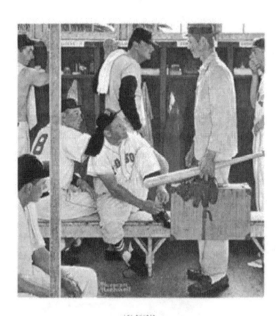

The Rookie

Chapter 11: Amazing Accomplishments
What's on your resumé?

Conversations

Writing a resumé can be challenging, since you want to present yourself well to a prospective employer, but you don't want to brag or inflate your accomplishments. Divide into groups or pairs and discuss the following:

1. What are employers looking for in a resumé?

2. What important characteristics or qualifications may be overlooked?

3. In your opinion, which of the following is true? Why?
    a. The man makes the job.
    b. The job makes the man.
4. Have you ever attended a job fair? If so, share your experience.

Social Situations

Attending a business lunch

Sooner or later, you will be invited to a business lunch. There are certain protocols that ought to be followed in order to leave a positive impression.

Do's	Don'ts
1. Be prompt—arrive early	1. Slurp your soup
2. Greet lunch partners with firm handshake	2. Eat large pieces of food
3. Turn off cell phone	3. Talk with food in your mouth
4. After being seated, place napkin in lap	4. Rush into business talk
5. Wait until all are served before eating	5. Eat too fast or too slowly
6. Give attention to those at your table	6. Expect another to pay unless they invited you
7. Use silverware from outside in	7. Take home leftovers if you don't pay
8. Say please and thank you	8. Cut all your meat at once
9. Treat restaurant staff with respect	9. Forget to send a thank-you note

Discuss with your classmates and teacher other rules of lunch etiquette. Then try to practice them at every lunch until they become second nature to you.

Pronunciation

Minimal pairs: Say these with a partner.

s	sh
sad	shad
sew	show
sort	short
sin	shin
sip	ship
save	shave
sign	shine
seep	sheep
sue	shoe
seat	sheet
sore	shore

Tongue Twisters: Repeat each sentence or phrase several times. Then say them quickly several times.
  a. She sells seashells by the sea shore.
  b. Shy Shelly says she shall sew sheets.

Perception: Idioms, phrasals, culture clues

Idioms in context: Listen to the dialog below and underline any unfamiliar terms.

Pat: Great lunch meeting! You sure did a super job planning it!

Sandi: Thanks. But I didn't think it went that well. **I worked like a beaver** to **cover all the bases**, but some things just **slipped through the cracks**.

Pat: What do you mean? The food was great; the mood was positive; and everyone seemed engaged in the meeting. Why are you so **worked up** about this?

Sandi: Well, you don't know all the **legwork** that went into the lunch. I met with the restaurant manager three times to **iron out** details, but still they didn't get it right. They bought the wrong hors d'oeuvers. They forgot to have decaf tea; and they didn't offer vinegarette dressing for the salad.

Pat: Good grief, Sandi! You're a perfectionist! **Don't sweat the small stuff!** I didn't even notice any of these **gaffes**. The important thing is that the meeting accomplished our goals, and our co-workers all seemed to be **on board** with the project. Don't worry. Everything will **work out for the best.**

Sandi: I guess you're right. You know, your encouraging words are **working wonders**. I really feel better about the whole thing. But now I guess we'd better **get down to work**.

Pat: There you go! But maybe you're becoming too uptight about this job. After work, why don't we go biking for an hour or so? You know the old saying: "**All work and no play makes Jack a dull boy.**"

New expressions: Idioms and Phrasals

What do you think these might mean?
How can you use them in your own conversations?

- worked like a beaver
- cover all the bases
- slipped through the cracks
- worked up
- legwork
- iron out
- Don't sweat the small stuff.
- gaffes
- on board
- work out for the best
- working wonders
- get down to work
- too uptight
- All work and no play makes Jack a dull boy

Collocations: Write and discuss situations where these are used.

work	**job**	
workout	cushy job	hold down a job
work out	menial job	out of a job
workshop	blue-collar job	take on the job of
legwork	white-collar job	on the job

Culture clues: Competition

Tied with individualism, "doing," and personal improvement, Americans also tend to value competition in almost every realm of life. Parents enroll their young children in many sports, both individual and team. While some children may just enjoy the activity, often the parents become fiercely competitive to the point of even yelling at the referees or judges and demanding decisions that would elevate their own child's status. On occasion, parents are asked to leave the sporting event because of their unsportsman-like conduct. To such parents, competition is more important than enjoyment, exercise, or skill development.

Competition is visible in the retail world, where one business will lower prices (or raise them) to keep up with a neighboring business. When one airline began charging for carry-on baggage, most of the others did likewise so that they wouldn't lose out on potential profits. Some retail stores even have a policy of matching competitors' advertised prices in order to keep customers loyal to the store.

Find a partner or two and discuss the following questions.

  a. What evidence of excessive competition have you observed?
  b. In your opinion, when and how is competition a positive factor? When and how does it become excessive?
  c. Do you think it is possible to be loyal to a team, a store, or a product without criticizing or belittling the competitor? If so, how? If not, why not?
  d. If you had children, would you enroll them in sports activities? How would you maintain a balance between intensity and fun?

 ## Listening and Bible Knowledge

Listening: Slang

Slang is an integral part of speech for many people. It differs from idioms in that slang often has a negative and/or crude connotation. Jonathon Green, in his introduction to Cassell's Dictionary of Slang, Second Edition, states:

"Slang is a counter-language. The language of the rebel, the outlaw, the despised, the marginal, the young. Above all, it is the language of the city—urgent, pointed, witty, cruel, capable of both excluding and including, of mocking and confirming."

You may hear slang frequently and wonder what it means. However, as an English language learner, you do not need to use it in order to be accepted. Much of slang is vulgar and demeaning, often with sexual overtones. Therefore, when you hear slang, you don't need to be concerned about its meaning. Just recognize from the context that the speaker chooses to use "shock-value" phrases that actually communicate a lack of sensitivity to the listener and a lack of manners.

We will deal with one example here. If you really feel the need to know the meanings of various slang phrases, look them up on the internet.   (www.wikianswers.com)

Question: What is the meaning of 'It sucks'?

Answer: "It sucks" is often used interjectionally in a bad situation. If a rock fell on your toe, you'd scream, "THAT SUCKS!" Or if you were watching a boring show on television, you'd say, "This show sucks!" or, alternatively, "This show sucks." Saying something "sucks" is somewhat vulgar, but very commonplace, even more so than curse words.

"It sucks" is a phrase usually said when a person does not like what he or she hears or sees. The word "suck" should not be used very often. It is often considered vulgar or improper.

Examples:
"I suck at bowling" might be used by somebody who says he is not good at bowling.
"I think you suck at Algebra" might be used by a person that thinks that his is not good at Algebra.

Bible Knowledge

 **Jesus Demonstrates His Power**

LORD over Everything

At a wedding feast in Cana of Galilee, it was traditional to serve the freshest wine first, reserving sour wine for the end of a feast. Jesus and his disciples and his mother were invited to a wedding feast when the host ran out of wine. Mary suggested to the servants to do whatever Jesus told them to do.

Jesus told the servants to fill six water-pots of stone containing twenty or thirty gallons apiece with water, then to draw out some and take it to the master of the feast. The master of the feast did not know the origin of the wine and said to the bridegroom, "You have saved the good wine for the end of the feast!" But the servants knew of the origin of the water turned into wine as a miracle by Jesus when He manifested His glory, and His disciples believed in Him.

As many people followed Jesus, He got into a boat with His disciples. Suddenly a great tempest arose on the Sea of Galilee so that the waves covered the boat, but Jesus was sleeping. The disciples woke Him saying, "LORD, save us! We are perishing!" But He said to them, "Why are you fearful and have such little faith?" He got up and rebuked the winds and the sea, and there was a great calm.

The men marveled saying, "Who can this be that even the wind and the sea obey Him?"

On the east side of the Sea of Galilee in the Gentile area of Gadarenes, a demon-possessed man came out of cave-tombs, and they were so exceedingly fierce that no one could pass that way. The demons cried out, "What have we to do with you, Jesus, You Son of God? Have you come here to torment us before the time? If you cast us out, please allow us to go into that whole herd of swine," as there was a herd of swine feeding a short distance from them. Jesus commanded the demons to leave and they entered the pigs; and suddenly the whole herd of swine ran violently down the steep place into the sea and perished in the water. Those who kept the pigs fled and ran into the city and told everything that had happened to the demon-possessed man. The whole city came out to meet Jesus and begged Him to leave their region.

As Jesus was teaching on a certain day, there were Pharisees and teachers of the Law sitting close by who had come from every town of Galilee, Judea, and Jerusalem. Since there was a huge crowd surrounding Jesus, men who wanted to bring a paralyzed man to Jesus could not get through the crowd. So they went up on the flat-roofed house-top, dug up the tiling and lowered the man with his bed into the midst before Jesus.

When Jesus saw their faith, He said to the man, "Man, your sins are forgiven you." The Scribes and the Pharisees accused Jesus of blasphemies because they knew that only God can forgive sins. Jesus perceived their thoughts and said to them, "That you may know that the Son of Man has power on earth to forgive sins, I told the man to take up his bed and go to his house." Immediately the man got up and glorified God as he went to his house, and the people were all amazed as they also glorified God and were filled with fear regarding the strange things they saw that day.

Jesus raised from the dead the only son of a widow. Jesus had compassion on the widow and said to her, "Do not weep!" Jesus touched the open coffin and said, "Young man, arise!" He, who had been dead, sat up and began to speak. Jesus presented the young man to his widowed mother. Fear came upon all and they glorified God saying, "A great Prophet has risen among us," and "God has visited His people."

A ruler came and worshipped Jesus and asked Jesus to raise up his daughter who had just died. On the way to the ruler's house, a woman, who for twelve years had a flow of blood, came from behind Jesus and touched the hem of His garment, hoping to be made well. Jesus said to her, "Be of good cheer, daughter, for your faith has made you well." And the woman was made well from that hour.

When Jesus came into the ruler's house, flute players and a noisy crowd wailed and ridiculed Jesus when he suggested to them that the daughter was sleeping. He put the crowd outside before He took her hand and raised her up. This report went everywhere.

---

*SIGNS and WONDERS—Jews sought for signs and wonders. The Apostle John selected seven signs from the many that Jesus performed to give evidences that Jesus was who He said He was—the Messiah of Israel, the Christ of God (John 4:25, 26)

Key Word = "believe" used 98 times

The Seven Signs (Miracles) of John's Gospel	Realms of Authority
1. Water to wine (2:1-11)	Quality
2. Healing the Nobleman's son (4:46-54)	Space
3. Healing man at pool (5:1-18)	Time
4. Feeding the five thousand (6:1-14)	Quantity
5. Walking on the water (6:16-21)	Nature
6. Healing the blind man (9:1-41)	Misfortune
7. Raising Lazarus (11:1-44)	Death

Discussion: Part 1

1. Prophets came first, followed by the greater Son of God. How does the miracle of the wine match the greatness of the last over the first?

2. What does the Bible teach about caring for the widow? How did Jesus help provide for the needs of the widow in this account? Why do you think He cared?

3. What is more important than the signs and wonders that Jesus did? Why? What is most important in our day and age?

4. What was the main concern of the Scribes and Pharisees? Do they seem to be genuinely concerned about people?

Part 2: Feeding the Five-Thousand

Jesus continued to heal people in Cana of Galilee but He began to detect that people only wanted to see signs and wonders. Jesus said, "He who hears My Word and believes in Him who sent Me has everlasting life…Just as the Father has life in Himself, so He gave the Son life in Himself and has given Him authority. I do not seek My own will but the will of the Father who sent Me."

Jesus then said that while He appreciated the witness of John the Baptizer, "I have a greater witness than John's, for the Father Himself is My witness, and the Father has given Me His works to finish…The Scriptures also testify of Me and Moses wrote about Me."

After this, Jesus and His disciples departed to a deserted place in the boat over the Sea of Galilee by themselves so that they could rest awhile. A great multitude followed Him from the cities because they saw His miracles. Jesus was moved with compassion for the people because they were like sheep without a Shepherd, so He taught them many things and healed their sick.

When evening came, Jesus' disciples wanted to send the people away to the surrounding towns and villages to buy food for themselves, but Jesus said, "They do not need to go away...Give them something to eat."

Because the Passover Feast was near, Jesus said to Philip, "Where shall we buy enough bread so that all these people may eat the Passover Feast?" Philip answered, "Eight months' wages would not buy enough bread for each one to have a bite!"

Jesus then asked them to determine how much food was available. Andrew said, "There is a lad here who has five barley loaves and two small fish, but what are they among so many people?" Jesus said, "Bring them to Me."

Because there was clean grass in the area, Jesus said, "Seat the people!" They sat in ranks of hundreds and in fifties and the number were about five-thousand men, besides woman and children.

Then Jesus took the loaves and looking up to heaven, He blessed and broke the bread and gave the loaves to His disciples and the disciples distributed the food to the seated people, and likewise the fish—as much as they wanted. When they were filled, Jesus told the disciples to gather up the fragments and there were twelve (12) basketfuls left over.

Those who saw this sign said, "This is truly the Prophet who is to come into the world." When Jesus perceived that the people wanted to force Him to be their king, Jesus sneaked away alone into the mountain to pray while He sent away His disciples, for they had not understood about the loaves because their hearts were hardened.
(Matthew 14:13-21, Mark 6:30-44 and 52, John 5:24-47, John 6)

After Jesus fed more than five thousand people and sent away the multitude, He sent His disciples in the boat to the other side of the lake—to Bethsaida, and He went alone to the mountain to pray.

When it was evening, the boat was in the middle of the sea and Jesus was alone on the land. Jesus saw the disciples straining at rowing for the wind was against them.
Before dawn after they had rowed about five or six kilometers, Jesus walked on the sea as though to pass ahead of the disciples, but the disciples saw Him walking on the sea and supposed it was a ghost, and they all saw Him and cried out and were troubled!

Immediately Jesus talked with them, "Take courage! It is I. Do not be afraid!"

Peter called to Jesus, "LORD, if it's You, tell me to come to you on the water."

"Come!" Jesus said. Peter got out of the boat and walked on the water toward Jesus, but as the wind whipped around him, he became afraid and began to sink and cried out, "Lord, save me!" Immediately Jesus reached out His hand and caught him and said, "Why did you doubt? You have little faith."

Then Jesus got into the boat with them and the wind ceased. They were completely scared out of their wits, and they wondered and were amazed…for since they hadn't understood the earlier miracle, how could they understand this one? (Matthew 14:22-33, Mark 6:45-56, John 6:15-710

Discussion: Part 2

1. What Old Testament story does this remind you of?

2. Do you think there is any significance that this event happened at Passover time?

3. Why did the people want to make Jesus king?

4. Why do you think Jesus resisted the idea of becoming king? Wasn't He born "King of the Jews?"

5. Jesus defied nature when He walked on the sea. How did He do this? If you were Peter, how would you have responded to Jesus' command, "Come"?

Assignment

1. What do you think are the strong points you could put on a résumé? What areas need improvement? What can you do now to strengthen your résumé?

2. Do a self-evaluation or ask a friend to evaluate your English pronunciation and word usage? What areas need more practice? Ask your teacher or a classmate to help.

3. Develop a list of words or phrases that are puzzling to you. Either investigate their meanings on the internet or ask your teacher. What guidelines can you employ to determine whether or not you should use these words or phrases?

4. Jesus accomplished many miracles while He was here on earth. Read the accounts listed in the section entitled "Signs and Wonders." How would you explain these events?

5. If you are interested in understanding Christianity more completely, start a notebook of questions and notes on preaching messages or Bible study discussions. Feel free to ask your teacher or pastor about things that puzzle you. Ask God to help you truly understand the message of His Word, the Bible.

Jesus Preaching the Sermon on the Mount

by James Tissot

Happy Birthday, Miss Jones
by Norman Rockwell

Chapter 12: The Master Teacher
What makes an outstanding teacher?

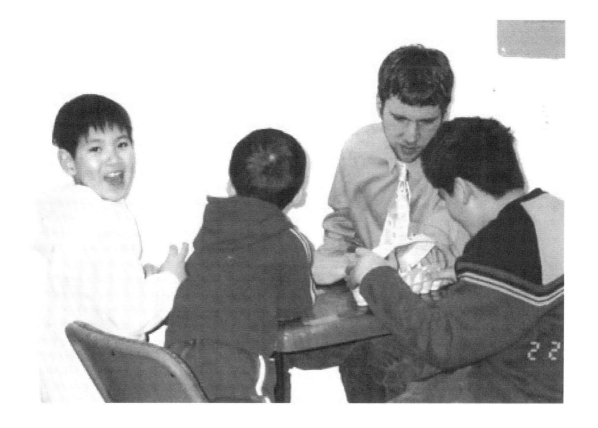

Conversations: Your Favorite Teacher

1. Think back on your educational experience. Who was your favorite teacher? Why? Have you kept in contact?

2. Do you think people are born teachers, or are they developed? Give reasons for your opinion.

3. Some countries provide special education for those interested in skilled labors jobs such as electrician, plumber, or auto mechanic. In your country, what training is available for those who do not want to attend college? Please describe the training.

4. In your country, what is the parents' role in education? Would you say it is active or passive? Please explain.

Social Situations: Parent Teacher Conferences

Most American schools conduct meetings between teachers and parents at least once a semester. The goal is to improve communication in order to develop cooperative efforts that will maximize the student's progress. The conference usually lasts 15-20 minutes, so it is beneficial to prepare specific questions before the meeting.

The first parent-teacher conference is usually held in October, so a parent might want to discuss such things as (1) skills to be mastered, (2) evaluation techniques, (3) peer relationships, (4), involvement in the child's academic progress, (5) problems or concerns the child has mentioned, (6) enrichment activities, (7) special help.

If you were the teacher, how might you encourage parents to become more involved in the child's education? If you were the parent, what concerns might you raise? How can you do that tactfully to created/maintain a positive relationship with the teacher?

Discussion groups or team meetings

University classes often require attendance at discussion groups. Businesses may have "team meetings," in which employees and supervisors meet to strategize, evaluate, clarify, and plan. Internationals are sometimes uncomfortable and intimidated by such meetings.

1. What are some factors that contribute to such discomfort or fear?

Pronunciation

Minimal pairs: j / y Practice these with a partner.

j	y
jet	yet
jeer	year
jarred	yard
jot	yacht
Jello	yellow
Jack	yak
Jess	yes
gel	yell
joke	yoke
jail	Yale
juice	use

Perception: Idioms, phrasals, culture clues

Idioms in context: Listen to the dialog below and underline any unfamiliar terms.

Scott: Can you believe that Dr. Ellis? Most of my profs (professors) are from **the old school**, but this guy's creativity is **off the charts**!

Seth: Yeah! I thought this would be another boring history class. **Boy**, was I wrong! American Cultural History is fascinating!

Scott: He sure **covers a lot of ground** in an hour and a half. He has **a real knack** for **connecting the dots** between art, music, literature, and the current events of the time period. I never realized they were even remotely related.

Seth: Some profs seem to come out of their **Ivy League ivory towers** to teach a class, then return to their little **world of academia**, totally disconnected from the real world. This guy is part instructor, part actor, part motivator. He's so totally unpredictable that I wouldn't dream of **cutting a class**! I can't wait to see what will happen next!

Scott: **Where in the world** does he **come up with** his ideas, anyway? Take, for example, the Hudson River School. The only Hudson River school I knew of was West Point. But Dr. Ellis showed us that these painters of the 1820's not only established an art genre, but also reflected the writers and events of the day.

Seth: And how about James Fenimore Cooper? Cooperstown is the home of the Baseball Hall of Fame, but who knew that it was the home of one of America's first popular writers? When "The Last of the Mohicans" came out as a movie, I had no idea it was based on Cooper's book set during the French and Indian War. **Man**! I'm learning so much!

Scott: So we walk into the classroom, and here is Dr. Ellis, pacing back and forth on the platform, somberly quoting the Native American leader:
> "The **pale faces** are masters of the earth, and the time of the **red men** has not yet come again. My day has been too long. In the morning I saw the sons of Unamis happy and strong; and yet, before the night has come, I have lived to see the last warrior of the wise race of the Mohicans."

You could almost picture the old chief mourning the loss of his entire tribe.
Dr. Ellis **sent shivers up my spine**!

Seth: Me, too! And at the same time Cooper was writing about the Indians, the enterprising Robert Fulton was building a canal to connect New York City with Buffalo, and then with the whole western frontier. I heard Bruce Springsteen sing "Low Bridge," but I didn't really picture the Erie Canal that was **changing the face of** America. I wish my high school history teacher had been so creative.

Scott: Yeah. Dr. Ellis makes you want to **crack the books**, and even go to the art museums.

Scott: Art museums? Now that might be **stretching it**--though I wouldn't mind visiting the Fenimore Art Museum next time I'm in Cooperstown. Did you know there's an Erie Canal Village in Rome, New York? You can even take a packet boat ride there. Hey, I'm starting to sound like a history fanatic. You can credit Dr. Ellis. He's **one in a million!**

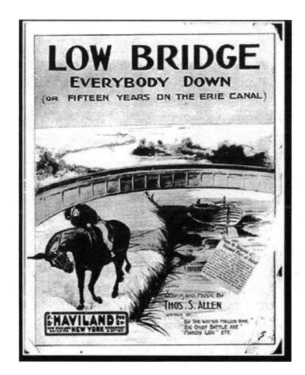

New expressions: Idioms

What do you think these might mean?
How can you use them in your own conversations?

the old school	come up with
off the charts	Man! Boy!
covers a lot of ground	pacing back and forth
real knack for	pale faces
connecting the dots	red men
Ivy League	sent shivers up my spine
ivory towers	changing the face of
world of academia	crack the books
cutting a class	stretching it
where in the world	one in a million

Phrasals and collocations

Phrasals

come up with	read off
come out with	read up on
come out of the woodwork	read out
come on	read into
drop in	call in
drop out	call for
drop over	call on
drop down	call off

Collocations

learning curve	teach collaboratively
learning impaired	team teach
rote learning	teach to the test
distance learning	teach intuitively
passive learning	teach competently

Culture clues: Homeschooling

"For much of history and in many cultures, enlisting professional teachers (whether as tutors or in a formal academic setting) was an option available only to a small elite. Thus, until relatively recently, the vast majority of people were educated by parents (especially during early childhood) and in the context of a specific type labor that they would pursue in adult life, such as working in the fields or learning a trade." It has only been since the early and mid 19th century that the formal classroom has been the most common form of education.

Public schools are not the only educational option for parents. Some send their children to private schools which may be classified as parochial, religious, military, or classical. Others educate their children at home. A homeschooling movement began in the late 1960's and early 1970's, prompted in part by perceived failures of traditional public schools and by growing research regarding the way young children learn. Some parents were also motivated to teach their children at home due to the changing morality of the 70's and the demise of traditional Judeo-Christian ethics in American society.

By 2006 an estimated 1.5 to 2 million school children in the United States received their education through a home school. Each state has its own homeschooling regulations, some of which address mandatory attendance, testing, supplying lesson plans, and graduation requirements. Parents who choose to homeschool make a huge commitment of time and energy, but do so with the expectation that their children will benefit in multiple ways by following this educational route.

Choose a partner and discuss the following:
1. What would be some advantages of homeschooling?
2. What would be some disadvantages?
3. How might parents compensate for the disadvantages?
   (www.wikipedia.org/wiki/homeschooling)

 ## Listening and Bible Knowledge

Listening: Acronyms

American English is filled with words that are actually acronyms (words formed from the initial letter or letters of a compound term). For example, the word NATO actually means North Atlantic Treaty Organization. When native English speakers use such terms, they assume the listeners know the meanings.

Acronyms relating to the computer or technology world are more common; and text messaging has brought the use of acronyms and abbreviations to a whole new level. However, it may be of benefit to learn the meanings of some common acronyms so that when you hear them, they will not disturb your ability to grasp the rest of the conversation.

Military	Education	Business	General
WAC	GMAT	TEAM	ASAP
SWAT	ISBN	BOGO	NIMBY
JAG	WiFi	REM	AARP
CAP	ERIC	OPEC	WASP
RADAR	TESOL	GEICO	ZIP
SOP	FAPE	SKU	RIP

ACRONYM ANSWERS :

Military:

SWAT=Special Weapons and Tactic
WAC=weapon aiming computer
JAG=Judge Advocate General
CAP=Civil Air Patrol
RADAR=radio detection and ranging
SOP=standard operating procedure

Business

TEAM=Time, Energy and Money
BOGO=Buy One, Get One
REM=Rapid Eye Movement
OPEC=Organization of Petroleum
          Exporting Countries
GEICO= Government Employees
          Insurance Company

General

ASAP=As Soon As Possible
NIMBY=Not In My Back Yard
AARP=American Association of Retired
          Persons
WASP=White Anglo Saxon Protestant
ZIP=Zone Improvement Plan
SKU=Stock Keeping Unit
RIP=Rest In Peace
WiFi=Wireless Fidelity

Education

GMAT=Graduate Management Admission Test
ISBN=International Standard Book Number
ERIC=Educational Research Informational
          Clearinghouse
TESOL=Teaching English to Speakers of Other
          Languages
FAPE=Families and Advocates Partnership for
          Education

 Bible Knowledge

Part 1: Jesus Taught about His Identity

As Jesus launched His public ministry, He traveled and lived among the people, teaching them formally in the Temple at Jerusalem and informally on varied occasions.   He performed many miracles and demonstrated that He was who He said He was—the Messiah of Israel, the Christ of God. Could it be that He truly was the long-awaited Deliverer promised back in the Garden of Eden?

Jesus, the master teacher, used object lessons and stories to maximize teaching impact on His followers as well as those who listened primarily out of curiosity. He addressed present realities of life, such as:

    Relationships   Love
    Pride   Humility
    Attitudes   Obedience
    Thankfulness   Wealth
    Service

The Gospel of Matthew and the Gospel of Luke contain many of Jesus' stories and parables, which were designed to move from real life circumstances to spiritual truth and people's need to repent of their sins and believe on Christ as their Deliverer. Jesus spoke about a bride and bridegroom, rich farmers, poor servants, a father and his wayward son, a lost coin, a good neighbor, and many other subjects.

The Gospel of John records accounts of Jesus' interactions with His disciples, with religious rulers, rich and poor, educated and uneducated, leaders and outcasts. In all His encounters, He pointed people to the Creator God and their need for personally trusting in Him. John the Baptist challenged the crowds to "behold the Lamb of God who takes away the sin of the world" (John 1:12). Before Israel had experienced the first Passover in Egypt, an innocent lamb had to be slain as a symbol of faith and obedience. Now the Lamb of God was to sacrifice His own life and shed His own blood so that people from every nation could experience God's forgiveness and be rescued from death.

Discussion: Part 1

1. Do you know any mono-cultural groups (such as Jews in this story) who believe their culture is the most important in the world?
2. How did Jesus capture interest in order to teach spiritual truths?
3. What was the goal of His teachings?

Part 2: Jesus Further Revealed Himself to the People

One day Jesus chose to travel through Samaria, a land of "half-breeds," Jews who had intermarried with other people groups and were thus despised by traditional Jews. At noon, the hottest part of the day, while His disciples went into the city to purchase food, Jesus encountered a Samaritan woman who had come at this unusual time to draw water from the well. As He spoke with her, He made clear that He was, indeed, the Messiah, and that He could give her "living water."

This woman knew of the Promised Deliverer and surely also knew how God had miraculously provided the nation of Israel with water in the wilderness as they escaped from Egypt. Through this unusual encounter with the woman at the well, many Samaritans met Jesus and believed that He was the Savior and Redeemer promised so long ago by God. (You can read this true account in John chapter 4.)

In the Old Testament, God had led Israel through the wilderness with a cloud by day and a pillar of fire by night. Jesus proclaimed, "I am the light of the world. He who follows Me shall not walk in darkness, but have the light of life" (John 8:12).

God provided manna to sustain Israel in the wilderness. This bread from heaven nourished and strengthened them all during their long journey to the Promised Land. Now Jesus taught, "I am the bread of life. He who comes to Me shall never hunger, and he who believes in Me will never be thirsty" (John 6:35-51).

****

While the seven miracles record the greatest of Jesus' work, the "I AM's" capture the essence of Jesus identity (His person) through His own Words.   The passages below are word pictures that reveal who Jesus Christ is.

The Seven "I AM's" in John's Gospel reflect in part Exodus 3:14—"I AM WHO I AM."

"I Am the Bread of Life"	John 6:35, 48
"I AM the Light of the World"	John 8:12; 9:5
"I AM the Good Shepherd" (Door of the sheep)	John 10:9-11
"I Am the Son of God"	John 10:36
"I AM the Resurrection and the Life"	John 11:25
"I Am the Way, Truth, Life"	John 14:6
"I AM the True Vine"	John 15:1

John 8:58—"Before Abraham was, I AM."

Jesus clearly revealed to the people of His day and to all succeeding generations that He is the Promised Deliverer, the One who can restore a person's relationship with his Creator God through repentance and faith in Christ.

Discussion: Part 2

1. Contrast physical water with spiritual water. What do you think Jesus meant by spiritual water? Did this woman finally receive the spiritual water? How do you know?
2. Who was Jesus' most effective contact person for impacting people in Samaria? Does that surprise you? Why or why not? Would that work in your culture?
3. Read John 14:1-6 and explain Jesus' response to Thomas.

Assignment

1. What skill or interest would you like to pursue, other than your job or education? Research local organizations that help develop such skills (ex. photography, camping, bird-watching, playing a musical instrument). Contact the group and plan to attend a meeting. Report your experience to our class.

3. Another educational alternative for young people is KIPP—Knowledge Is Power Program—which establishes public charter schools in low-performing districts. Do some research on KIPP and write a summary of the program, including the positive and negative sides of this type approach. You may want to include a video clip if possible.

3. One of the most widely repeated parables of Christ is found in Luke 10:25-37. Read this section of Scripture; then retell it in your own words. Perhaps you would like to act it out with some classmates. Gather necessary props; assign parts; then perform the story for the rest of the class.

4. Create a pictorial collage of the "I am" statements in the Gospel of John. Prepare to share the significance of each illustration.

Federal Building in **Oklahoma City bombing.**

Timothy McVey

**World Trade Center
September 11**

Khalid Sheikh Mohammed

Chapter 13: Parades, Plots, and Problems
What kinds of difficulties do famous people face?

Conversations: From Popularity to Ruin

Throughout history, people have risen to prominence, only to be destroyed by others, by greed, by personal ambition, or by unwise choices. One ancient writer said, "How the mighty have fallen!"

1. Think of an entertainer, sports star, or other well-known person who seemed to be on the way to lifetime success, then did or said something that greatly changed his/her future. Tell your classmates about that person.
2. Why do you think such falls from popularity happen? Could they be avoided?
3. What part does jealousy from the competition play in such career crashes?
4. Can you think of an incident in history in which the fallen person was not guilty of bad decisions or of a crime, but was nevertheless treated as a villain?

 # Social Situations: Attending a funeral

The ultimate career-stopper is death. Everyone faces it. It's difficult to know what to do or say at a time of loss. If you have occasion to attend a funeral in this country, it might be helpful to know some of the common customs and etiquette for such an occasion.

1. Visitation, calling hours, or wake are terms for the opportunity to be with the grieving family and express your sympathy. This event may take place in a funeral home or place of worship prior to the service. The casket containing the body of the deceased is present, and may be either open or closed, at the decision of the family. Flowers, which are given by relatives, friends, and business acquaintances, are on display around the casket. Family members receive visitors and their expressions of sorrow. There is no need to refrain from crying, which is a normal expression of sorrow.

2. The funeral or memorial service is a public event (usually) at which relatives, friends, colleagues, neighbors, and other acquaintances gather to honor the deceased. A pastor or other religious leader may lead the service, offering verses of comfort and prayers for the family. Often family and friends will say a few words of remembrance, share a special memory, perhaps even sing. Sometimes a video or slide presentation with photos of the deceased will be shown.

3. The burial usually follows the funeral service. Those who wish to go to the cemetery drive in a slow funeral procession to the burial site. After a few words and prayer, every one departs, with the family staying longest. Sometimes each person places a flower on the casket before returning to his car and leaving. The family may or may not choose to watch the casket lowered into the ground.

4. It is common to have a meal for the family and close friends following the burial. This may be held in a home, a church or other facility.

5. Common questions:
    a. What do I wear? While black has been the traditional color of mourning in the west, that is not a requirement. Generally a dark or subdued color is appropriate, Conservative dress is always safe.
    b. What do I say? Less is sometimes best. Express your sorrow over the loss, what this person meant to you, how much you respected the deceased. Keep it simple. If you are comfortable with giving hugs, a hug sometimes says a lot. If family members want to talk about the deceased, be a good listener.
    c. Do I send or give a gift? Friends will often send flowers. A food basket sent to the family home is welcomed, as is a casserole, baked goods, or fruit. It is not necessary to send anything, but if you feel you'd like to help, these are appreciated. Sometimes the obituary will state, "in lieu of flowers, gifts may be given to…" a charitable organization.
    d. What do I do during the funeral service? Seat yourself somewhere behind the first few rows, which are reserved for family. Listen with respect to the speaker. Be sure your cell phone or pager is turned off!

Your presence can be a real encouragement to the family, so do not hesitate to attend, even though it may be your first funeral in this country.

 ## Pronunciation:

Minimal Pairs: sh/ch Practice these with a partner

sh	ch
cash	catch
ships	chips
bush	butch
leash	leech
wish	witch
shin	chin
wash	watch
shows	chose
sheets	cheats
shoe	chew
sheer	cheer

Perception: Idioms, phrasals, culture clues

Idioms in context: Listen to the dialog below and underline any unfamiliar terms.

Chad: What's the matter, Jake? You look **down in the dumps**.

Jake: Didn't you hear? **I fell fo**r a **ponzi scheme**! I've just lost almost all of my life savings!

Chad: You're kidding! What happened?

Jake: It's a long story. Are you sure you want to hear my **tale of woe**?

Chad: Of course? What are friends for? **A problem shared is a problem halved.**

Jake: O.K. Well, about six months ago a so-called friend, a business colleague, asked me to consider investing in his new securities company. It sounded great, so I checked with another colleague just to be sure this **company was legit**. Everything he told me was positive. He painted **a rosy picture** of success just waiting for me.

Chad: Didn't anyone ever tell you, "**If it sounds too good to be true, it probably is too good to be true?**"

Jake: Yeah, I know. But I actually believed this guy. He turned out to be **a Judas**. Big time!

Chad: So you **got in over your head**? How much did you lose?

Jake: Too much! This whole company is a scam, and I fell for it. **I dug my own grave** by not conferring with someone outside our office. These two colleagues were **in cahoots** with each other. They flat-out lied! They probably laughed as I saw my investments suddenly **go south**. And they **made a killing** in the process!

Chad: Bernie Madoff all over again, huh? So what are you going to do about it?

Jake: Well, I just found out that a lot of other people were also **suckered into** this scheme, and they're filing a lawsuit. I think I'll join them. They want to **get to the bottom** of this problem, and so do I.

Chad: I wish you well, pal. I hope these guys get caught and thrown into jail. Then they can **stew in their own juices**, and maybe you can recover at least some of your losses.

Jake: Thanks. I hope so, too. I can't believe I was that gullible.

New expressions: Idioms

What do you think these might mean? How can you use them in your own conversations?

down in the dumps
fell for
my tale of woe
the company was legit
rosy picture
a Judas
got in over your head

I fell for it
I dug my own grave
in cahoots
go south
made a killing
suckered into this scheme
get to the bottom
stew in their own juices

Collocations: plot, kill, bury

plot against
plot out
plot of ground
plot on
plot twists
The plot thickens.

make a killing
killjoy
kill the fatted calf
kill time
kill your resume

bury your feelings
buried under
bury the hatchet
bury your differences
bury your head in a book
bury your face in your hands
dead and buried
buried treasure

Culture clues: Efficiency, practicality, bottom line

Since the Industrial Revolution of the 18th and 19th centuries, American values have reflected the changing economy. Moving from labor-intensive, finely crafted items to factory-built, mass-produced goods caused a shift in thinking toward efficiency and profit margins. Today many Americans seem greatly concerned with how fast they can obtain a product and how much it will cost.

With a partner discuss the following:
a. Which is more important, the product or the reasons behind wanting the product? Why? (example: HDTV, Wii)
b. "What's the bottom line?" is a frequently asked question. What do you think this phrase means? Is it used in any context other than a business transaction? Would you ask this question in your country?
c. In your opinion, are Americans too open in discussing the cost of goods and services? Compare or contrast this openness with your culture's approach to the subject.
d. If you could choose between a handcrafted piece of furniture or a mass-produced one, which would you choose? What factors would influence your decision?

Listening and Bible Knowledge

Listening: More Acronyms

The following words are actually acronyms commonly used in health, education, and general life. What do they mean? Try incorporating some of them in your daily conversations.

HVAC	HIPPA
NASA	FOB
PIN	HAZMAT
NASCAR	DOT
MOPS	AIDS

ACRONYM ANSWERS

HVAC=Heating, Ventilation, and Air Conditioning
HIPPA=Health Insurance Portability and Accountability Act
NASA=National Aeronautics and Space Administration
FOB=Forward Operating Base, Free on Board
PIN=Personal Identification Number
HAZMAT=Hazardous Materials
NASCAR=National Association for Stock Car Auto Racing
DOT=Department of Transportation
MOPS=Mothers of Pre Schoolers
AIDS=Acquired Immune Deficiency Syndrome
TARP=Troubled Asset Recovery Plan

Buzzwords are words or phrases connected with a specialized field, often related to technology or current trends. If you are unfamiliar with these buzzwords, you will have more difficulty listening and understanding the person using them. If you are currently using social networking to stay connected with friends, many will probably be familiar. If not, discuss the meanings with a classmate or teacher.

staycation	credit crunch	underemployed	donut hole
stimulus package	TARP	Tweet	Twitter
unfriend	Tweading	Twitterbox	app

Bible Knowledge

Part 1: Christ's Betrayal and Arrest

The triumphal entry into Jerusalem left the Jewish people excited. Surely Jesus was the promised King! They held an impromptu parade and hailed Him as the long-awaited Deliverer. Finally they would be rid of the Roman rulers, or so they thought. Little did they realize the strong undercurrent of opposition to Jesus.

Enemies rarely start out as enemies, yet from the time of Jesus' birth, people were determined to destroy Him. First, King Herod wanted to kill baby Jesus because others anticipated Jesus would become King of the Jews. At the start of His public ministry, Satan met Jesus In the wilderness and attempted to deter Him from His mission.

Jesus warned His disciples to beware of the Pharisees and Sadducees. They were religious leaders who took great pride in keeping small details of man-made law, but rejected God's commandments in the process.

Christ spoke openly to these leaders, accusing them of desiring the praise of man rather than the praise God. He did not soften His message to them. Consequently they sought opportunities to destroy Jesus.

 **Discussion: Part 1**

1. Why did King Herod want to kill Jesus?
2. What seemed to be the emphasis of the religious leaders? How did that differ from Christ's emphasis?

Part 2: Plots against Jesus

After approximately three years of preaching, teaching, and doing many miracles, Jesus knew that His life would soon end. The Lamb of God would give up His life to be the Deliverer promised to Adam and Eve so many years ago. While other Jews were preparing the Passover celebration, the chief priests and religious leaders were conspiring to arrest and execute Christ.

Jesus met with His disciples in an upper guestroom to prepare for the Passover. At that time He introduced the Lord's Supper, which He commanded His followers to observe until He comes again. During that final meal together (known as the Last Supper), Jesus was very troubled in His spirit and said, "One of you will betray Me." The disciples were perplexed. Who would think of betraying Jesus?

Jesus dipped the bread and gave it to Judas Iscariot, who asked, "Teacher, is it I?" Jesus replied, "You said it!" Then Jesus said to Judas, "What you do, do quickly!" The others did not know why Jesus said this, but thought that Jesus was sending Judas on an errand because Judas had the money box. Judas went out quickly into the night to complete the betrayal arrangements.

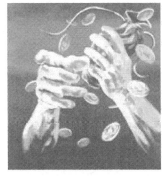

Jesus dearly loved His disciples, so He took this last opportunity to demonstrate an important concept: servant leadership. Jesus took a towel and prepared to wash His disciples' feet, a task for the household servant. Jesus said, "I am your Teacher and your Lord, yet I washed your feet. This is an example for you to be humble before others, for a servant is not greater than his master, nor am I greater than He who sent Me." Jesus was obedient to His Father and showed His obedience by serving others.

Jesus also spoke with them about His departure. Peter wanted to know where He was going and vowed to die for Christ. However, Jesus responded that in a few short hours, Peter would deny three times that he even knew Christ.

Jesus tried to calm His worried disciples and said to them, "Do not let your hearts be troubled. I go to prepare a place for you; then I will come again and receive you to Myself, that where I am, there you may be also."

"I am the way, the truth, and the life; no one comes to the Father except through Me."

 **Discussion: Part 2**

1. What do you think Judas was thinking about as he ate with Jesus?
2. What humbling act did Jesus do to teach His disciples an important lesson?
    In your country, do leaders show acts of service?
3. Whom or what did Jesus say He is? How might that claim affect you?

Part 3: Betrayal, Arrest, and Trial

After supper, Jesus went with His disciples to the Garden of Gethsemane, a place Judas Iscariot knew well. Deeply distressed, Jesus said to them, "My soul is extremely sad unto death. Stay here and be vigilant with Me."

Then Jesus went a little farther and fell on His face praying, "Father, all things are possible for You. If it's possible, let this fate that has been prepared for Me be removed. Yet, not as I will but as You will." He found His disciples asleep, but He continued praying so intensely that His perspiration became as drops of blood falling to the ground.

When He arose from prayer, He woke His disciples, who had fallen asleep and said, "Get up. My betrayer is near."

Even while Jesus was speaking, Judas Iscariot arrived at the garden with a large crowd of religious leaders armed with clubs and swords. Judas greeted Jesus saying, "Teacher! Teacher!" and kissed Him; but Jesus asked him, "Judas, are you betraying the Son of Man with a kiss?"

Immediately people from the crowd grabbed Jesus. Peter tried at first to defend Him, but soon the other disciples, fled away into the night, afraid of the rowdy crowd. Jesus was left alone with the angry leaders. Members of the crowd kindled a fire in the courtyard of the high priest's compound. Peter sat among them and warmed himself at the fire. Some of the crowd began to question Peter's relationship with Jesus, but he denied knowing Christ. Three times Peter insisted that he didn't know Jesus; then he heard a rooster crow. At that moment Jesus looked at Peter. Ashamed, Peter left and cried loudly, weeping for what he had done. It was just as Jesus had said!

The Jewish council, the Sanhedrin, tried to bring false witnesses against Jesus so that they could put Him to death, but their testimonies did not agree. Finally they asked, "Are you the Son of God?" Jesus replied, "Correct! I am!" The furious leaders condemned Him to death, though they had no evidence against Him. Then they led Jesus to Pilate, the Roman governor, asking for the death penalty.

Pilate interviewed Jesus but found no fault in Him. He knew that the chief priests had handed over Jesus because of envy, but the priests stirred up the crowd which demanded His death. Soldiers led Jesus into a hall filled with soldiers who twisted a crown of thorns and put it on His head. They put a scarlet robe on Him and mocked Him. They struck Him, spit on Him, and pretended to worship Jesus. Finally Pilate gave in to the pressures of the screaming crowd. He ordered the soldiers to beat Jesus with whips made of leather strips and sharp metal pieces; then he delivered Jesus to be put to death on a cross.

One day Jesus was hailed as a king. A few days later He was condemned as a criminal, though He had done nothing to deserve this death sentence.

Discussion: Part 3

1. Describe the scene in the Garden of Gethsemane. What part impacts you the most? Why?
2. Peter said that he would follow Jesus. Yet when pressures came, he denied the Lord. What kinds of pressures might make today's follower of the Lord be tempted to deny Christ?
3. Why do you think there was so much hatred from the religious leaders against Jesus?

Assignment

1. Everyone faces problems of different magnitudes. Some people desire counsel of friends or relatives, while others try to solve their problems alone. Think about a serious problem you have faced. How did you find a solution? Has it proven to be a good one? Why or why not?

2. One unique genre of American music is the Negro spiritual. As African slaves worked in the cotton fields of wealthy plantation owners, the slaves often sang about their struggles, their fears, and their hopes. Sometimes the lyrics of their songs had double meanings: one relating to the obvious, one hinting at their desire for freedom. Other lyrics were songs of worship that spoke of a better day, even though death might be the avenue of experiencing that better time.

    Read the lyrics; then try singing the song, "Swing Low, Sweet Chariot."

    Chorus:
    Swing low, sweet chariot,
    Comin' for to carry me home;
    Swing low, sweet chariot,
    Comin' for to carry me home.
    Verse 1:
    I looked over Jordan,
    And what did I see?
    Comin' for to carry me home,
    A band of angels comin' after me,
    Comin' for to carry me home.

    Chorus:
    Swing low, sweet chariot,
    Comin' for to carry me home;
    Swing low, sweet chariot,
    Comin' for to carry me home.
    Verse 2:
    If you get there before I do,
    Coming for to carry me home,
    Tell all my friends I'm comin' too,
    Comin' for to carry me home.

3. Research other Negro spirituals, such as "Nobody Knows the Trouble I Seen." Draw illustrations of the lyrics or write a summary of what you think the song is describing.

4. Choose a current event that centers on a significant problem—for a country, an individal, or a company. Interview several of your friends or classmates and ask them how they might solve this particular problem. Prepare a report to share with the class. (Examples: natural disaster, war, career loss, bankruptcy, dishonest business dealings, moral failure)

5. Read a Gospel account of Christ's betrayal and trial (Matthew 26-27, Mark 14, Luke 22, John 17-18). What additional details are included in these eye-witness reports? How do they affect your understanding of Jesus' life and work?

6. Paintings can convey a sense of action or emotion. Look at the following and write your reaction to the painting. How does it make you feel? What do you think will happen next? Grandma Moses: "The Thunderstorm"

7. Famous people sometimes fall from popularity due to their own choices. Choose a person of interest to you and research his or her fall from fame. Prepare a 3-5 minute speech that describes the "before, during, and after" aspects of this person's career plunge. Try to conclude with some lessons your listeners can learn for their own lives.

Assassination of Lincoln

Catching the Turkey by Grandma Moses

Chapter 14: Tragedy or Triumph
Is this the end or the beginning?

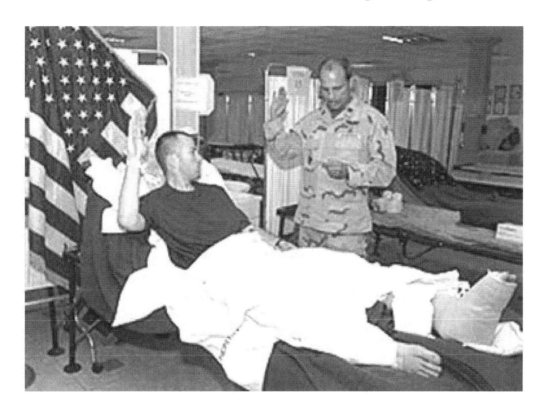

Conversations: Converting tragedy into triumph

1. Think back on a time that you or an acquaintance was going through a difficult time. What was the situation? Did anything good come from it? Explain.

2. Zig Zigler, well-known motivational speaker, said, "Failure is a detour, not a dead-end street." Do you agree or disagree? Why?

3. Some people believe that death is the final moment of a person's existence. Others believe there is life after death. What is the common belief in your country? What is your personal belief about death and life after death?

 Social Situations: Celebrating Easter

All around the world Christians celebrate the resurrection of Jesus Christ from the dead. This will be discussed in detail in the Bible Knowledge section. This holiday, called Easter, has both secular and sacred elements. You may be invited to share an Easter celebration with a family or at a church. This holiday may include one or more of the following elements:

1. Cantata
2. Passion Play
3. Sunrise service
4. Church service
5. Easter dinner
6. Family activities

a. Share what you know about these events.

b. Ask your teacher and classmates about the ones which are unfamiliar to you.

 Pronunciation:

Minimal pairs: g / k

gum	come	hog	hock
gave	cave	mug	muck
gold	cold	pig	pick
gash	cash	sag	sack
good	could	wig	wick

Vowel + r

ar	er	ir	or	ur
far	fer	fir	for	fur
bar	ber	bir	bore	burr
cart	person	first	more	hurt
farm	were	shirt	shore	curt

What do you notice about the sounds? Are they pronounced differently just because they are spelled differently?

 ## Perception: Idioms, phrasals, culture clues

Idioms in context: Listen to the dialog below and underline any unfamiliar terms.

Brian: Do you have a minute? I need some input for a project I'm considering.

Sara: Is it a **matter of life or death**?

Brian: Hardly! But it could impact many people in this city. The musical scene has been **kind of dead** lately, and I'd really like to **resurrect** the Community Orchestra and Chorale (COC). However, there are issues to resolve.

Sara: Like what?

Brian: Well, I've contacted a number of the musicians who previously participated. Several are really enthusiastic about **breathing new life into** the COC. They said they'd **drum up** more interest among their colleagues.

Sara: That's great So **what's the hitch**?

Brian: Well, Bob, the lead baritone who did such a fantastic job 3 years ago, is a wreck. Apparently he has had some family problems and has started skipping rehearsals. AND he's **hitting the bottle**—often. That may be the **kiss of death** for him.

Sara: Has anyone tried approaching Bob privately? Maybe he needs a **shoulder to cry on** and some counseling. He used to **bury himself in his work**. Now it sounds as though he's trying to **drown his sorrows** in a bottle. He needs help!

Brian: You've got a point. It's easier to consider him **dead in the water** than to intervene. Come to think of it, I do know someone who just might be able to **lend an ear**.

Sara: I hope so. Bob needs to **pull out of this slump** soon. It would be fantastic to get the COC ready for an Easter presentation of Handel's "Messiah." If Bob can **get his act together** in time, he can be singing "Hallelujah!" instead of **putting the final nails in his own coffin.**

Brian: Hey, Sara, thanks a bunch for the suggestion! I'll speak with my friend about Bob and see if he can talk some sense into the guy. Maybe Bob will **get a new lease on life**, and so will the COC. They really need him!

Sara: O.K. I'm going to stop by the ticket office and make reservations for the Easter concert!

New expressions:
What do you think these might mean? How can you use them in your own conversations?

matter of life or death	bury himself in his work
kind of dead	drown his sorrows
resurrect	dead in the water
breathing new life into	lend an ear
drum up	pull out of this slump
What's the hitch?	get his act together
hitting the bottle	putting the final nails in his own coffin
kiss of death	get a new lease on life
a shoulder to cry on	

Collocations and phrasals: death, hit, drop, roll, pull

at death's door	hit the books
cheat death	hit it off
dead to the world	It hit me.
dead meat	Take a hit.
	hit and run

roll in	drop in	pull in
roll over	drop over	pull over
roll out	drop out	pull out
roll back	drop back	pull back

Culture clues: Change as natural and positive

In some cultures, tradition is valued far above change. In America, change has been an integral part in the development of the country. New lands to explore, new cities to develop, new ideas, and technical innovations have all been natural and often positive. As westward expansion took place, the concept of "Manifest Destiny"—literally "known future"—became both popular and motivating.

While some families value certain traditions, those traditions seem to diminish with succeeding generations that embrace change and influence the future much more than traditions. Statements like, "The past is the past," and "You can't go back" influence people to make their world better as they work hard and use their intellect and skills to that end.

Choose a partner and discuss the following quotes by well known Americans.
Tell whether you agree or disagree and why. Consider how you may have seen the statement in action as you have observed your neighbors or co-workers.

a. Historian Henry Steele Commager: "Change does not necessarily assure progress, but progress implacably requires change."

b. Writer Ralph Waldo Emerson: "Nature is a mutable cloud which is always and never the same."

c. Politician Robert F. Kennedy: "Few will have the greatness to bend history itself; but each of us can work to change a small portion of events, and in the total of all those acts will be written the history of this generation."

d. Runaway slave Harriet Tubman: "Every great dream begins with a dreamer. Always remember, you have within you the strength, the patience, and the passion to reach for the stars to change the world."

e. Columnist George F. Will: "The future has a way of arriving unannounced."

Listening and Bible Knowledge

Listening: Fillers and Flags

Many English speakers punctuate their speech with a multitude of fillers—words with no particular significance. Examples are: **you know, like, well, wow, of course, uhuh, mmmm, uh, you know what I mean, there you go, exactly.** Language learners hear these fillers and in trying to process every word, lose out on the more important words of the sentence. Consciously recognize these annoying and unnecessary fillers, and discipline yourself to ignore them.

Flags, on the other hand, also add words to sentences, but may be quite useful as you begin to recognize their function. Listen for words or phrases that signify a transition of some sort, and practice incorporating them into your own speech. Once you understand their usage, these flags can actually speed up your listening and comprehending process. Examples of flags are: **to clarify, finally, in conclusion, first, second, what's more, however, but, on the other hand.**

When you hear such words or phrases, prepare your mind for a transition. Try utilizing them in your own speaking, and try expanding the list as you hear other "signal" words.

Bible Knowledge

Part 1: The Death of Jesus Christ

Death by crucifixion was personally humiliating and physically excruciating. The convicted criminal was forced to carry his own heavy cross through the streets and up the hill to Golgotha, the place of execution. Weak and bleeding from the cruel whipping, Jesus stumbled along the path, followed by a large crowd. Some mocked; others wept.

Roman soldiers ridiculed Jesus, gambled for his tunic, and then drove long, sharp spikes into his hands and feet, nailing Him to the cross. The pain must have been indescribable. Jesus' response was, "Father, forgive them, for they do not know what they are doing."

While Christ hung in agony on the cross, with a criminal on either side of Him, religious leaders mocked, sneered, and hurled insults at the sinless Son of God. At noon, intense darkness enveloped the land. As Jesus took upon Himself the sins of the people, He cried with a loud voice, "My God, My God, why have You forsaken Me?"

At this time, Jesus, knowing that all was finished so that the Scriptures might be fulfilled, said, "I am thirsty." Someone filled a sponge with sour wine and put it on a branch of hyssop, a bitter herb eaten with the Passover Supper. When Jesus had received it, He cried out with a loud voice, "It is finished!" With one final gasp of breath, Jesus spoke in a loud voice, "Father, into Your hands I commit My spirit." He bowed His head and gave up His spirit, breathing His last. It was precisely the time of the final sacrifice for the evening Passover. The Lamb of God had died.

At that very moment, the thick veil in the Temple split into two pieces from top to bottom; the earth quaked; and the rocks split. When the centurion and those with him who were guarding Jesus saw the earthquake, they were terrified and exclaimed, "Truly this was the Son of God."

 **Discussion: Part 1**

1. Observe the things that Jesus said while he was on the cross.
    List His words and tell why they were said or what events happened at that time.
2. What was the attitude of the soldiers as they crucified Jesus? Did that change? How?
3. If you had been in the crowd during Jesus' crucifixion, how do you think you might have responded?

Part 2: Christ's Burial

Jesus Christ was dead. Instead of being satisfied with their successful plot, religious leaders were more concerned about breaking religious laws than about unjustly putting to death the One who came to deliver them from sin. Because it was the preparation for the Sabbath, the Jews asked Pilate to assure that the three were dead by breaking their legs, so that the bodies could be removed from public before the start of the holy day. When the soldiers examined Jesus, they saw that He was already dead. Rather than breaking His legs, they pierced His side with a spear, and immediately blood and water gushed out. This was a fulfillment of Scriptures: "Not one of His bones shall be broken;" and, "They shall look on Him whom they pierced."

A man named Joseph from Arimathea boldly approached Pilate and asked permission to retrieve the body of Jesus. Joseph, accompanied by Nicodemus, took Jesus down from the cross and prepared Jesus' body for burial. They took strips of clean linen, combined with special spices, and wrapped the strips around His body like a cocoon.

In a garden near Golgotha, Joseph owned a new tomb that had been hewn out of the rock. The two men placed Jesus' body in the tomb, rolled a large stone against the entrance, and departed.

Women from Galilee followed Joseph and Nicodemus. Sitting opposite the tomb, they observed how Jesus' body was laid in the tomb. Then they returned home and prepared spices and fragrant oils for His burial. According to the commandment of Moses, the women rested on the Sabbath day.

 **Discussion: Part 2**

1. How did Joseph and Nicodemus put the burial cloth around Jesus? Was it in one piece or many strips? How does this help you understand the Shroud of Turin?
2. Describe Joseph and Nicodemus. What kind of men do you think they were?
3. What might be the significance of the temple veil splitting from top to bottom?
4. What proofs of Jesus' death are mentioned in the account?

Part 3: He's Alive

Some of the women who devotedly followed Christ took spices very early on the first day of the week to anoint Jesus' body. As they walked in the pre-dawn darkness, they discussed the challenge of removing the heavy stone from the tomb's entrance.

Meanwhile, a violent earthquake occurred at the tomb, for an angel of the Lord came from heaven, rolled back the stone, and sat on it. The guards were exceedingly frightened and fell to the ground motionless and powerless. When the women arrived, they were met by an angel who gave them a puzzling message.

"Why do you seek the living among the dead? Do not be afraid, for I know you are looking for Jesus the Nazarene who was crucified. He is not here for He has risen just as He said. Come! See the place where He lay. Then go quickly and tell His disciples and Peter. He is going ahead of you into Galilee. There you will see Him, just as I told you."

The women hurried back, trembling but joyful, to share this news with the disciples. At first they ridiculed the women, but later Peter and John ran to the tomb to investigate personally. They discovered the message was true; Jesus had risen as He said. Soon Mary Magdalene, then two men from Emmaus, then the other disciples witnessed firsthand the risen Christ, who spoke with them, ate with them, and reassured them that He was, indeed, alive.

During the next forty days over five hundred people saw Christ in His risen body and testified that He was alive, just as He had proclaimed. Though the religious leaders thought they had rid themselves of this troublesome Jesus, he proved by His resurrection that He has power over sin and death. John wrote in his gospel:

"…and there are also many other things that Jesus did, which, if they were written one by one, I suppose that even the world itself could not contain the books that would be written." (John 21:25 NKJV)

 **Discussion: Part 3**

1. Why do you think the chief priest requested additional security for the tomb?
2. What happened to the guards when the angel appeared?
3. Why didn't the apostles believe the women? Do you think you would have?
4. The disciples doubted at first that Jesus was alive. If you were there, how do you think you would have responded?

 # Assignment

1. Thanksgiving, Christmas, and Easter are three important American holidays. However, there are many more, including New Year's, Memorial Day, and Independence Day. Perhaps you celebrate similar holidays in your home country.
    a. Develop a presentation on one of your favorite holidays. Include some traditions, activities, family observances, music, and photos if possible.
    b. Prepare to share your report with the class.

2. Christ's death, burial, and resurrection are the inspiration for many musical compositions. George F. Handel actually directed his world famous "Messiah" as an Easter celebration, though it is often performed now at Christmas.
    a. Listen to Handel's "Messiah" in whole or in part, including the "Hallelujah Chorus."
    b. Write down some of the lyrics. Were these Handel's words, or did they come from another source?
    c. What is the overall spirit conveyed by this musical masterpiece?

3. Compare Handel's "Messiah" with Mahler's "Resurrection Symphony." What similarities and differences do you notice? Which piece do you prefer?

4. About four million people visit Arlington National Cemetery each year. Located in Arlington, VA, just outside Washington, DC, it is the burial place for America's veterans and war dead. Perhaps you have a similar cemetery in your country. Perhaps you have already visited Arlington.
    a. What are some of the reasons so many people visit this cemetery?
    b. What emotions does it evoke?
    c. Compose an original poem or draw an illustration that expresses the significance of such a place.

5. Read a Gospel account of Jesus' crucifixion, burial, and resurrection.
   Choose either   Matthew 26-28
                    Mark 14-16
                    Luke 22-24
                    John 13-21
   or read all four versions of these events. Write any questions you might have about these events.

6. There are several movies and DVDs related to the Easter story. Choose one of these, watch it, write your questions, and bring them to class to discuss.

    "The Robe"   "The Jesus Video"
    "God's Story"   "The Hope"
    "Ben Hur"   "The Greatest Story Ever Told"

7. One of the most famous Christian hymns about Jesus' death is "The Old Rugged Cross." You will find a copy on the next page. Read it and sing it with your class. Discuss any phrases that might be confusing to you. A famous Easter hymn follows that. Read, sing, and discuss that also.

The Old Rugged Cross

Boyhood Dreams by N.Rockwell

Compartment C, Car 193 by E. Hopper

Chapter 15: The Future
Where will you be 30 years from today?

Conversations:

1. What are your hopes and dreams for the next 10 years? The next 20 years?

2. Describe the kind of person you wish to be married to (if you want to be married).

3. If you want to remain single, would you want a roommate? Describe the ideal roommate?

4. What do you want to do when you retire? Where would you like to live after retiring?

5. Do you believe that you can control your future (your destiny)?

 Social Situations: Attending a party

Getting together with co-workers, classmates, and even strangers can be both enjoyable and stressful.

1. To eliminate as much stress a possible, discuss the following factors:
   a. How to respond to the invitation: RSVP, phone, email, mail
   b. Type of party: formal, informal, beach, picnic
   c. Whether or not to take a gift or food
   d. What to wear
   e. When to arrive and depart

2. How do the above factors compare with your home culture's practices?

 Pronunciation:

Minimal pairs   voiced th / d

th	d
those	doze
bathe	bade
breathing	breeding
heather	header
lather	ladder
worthy	wordy
other	udder
father	fodder

Intonation: Commands vs questions

Commands (imperatives) usually start with a verb and end with emphasis or stress on the last word. The inflection at the end of the sentence is falling.

Questions, on the other hand, are usually more wordy and end with a rising inflection. Listen to your teacher read the following sentences, then repeat, trying to copy the voice inflection.

    a. Wash the dishes.
       Would you please wash the dishes?

    b. Finish your vegetables.
       Would you please finish your vegetables?

    c. Don't text while you're driving.
       Would you please stop texting while you're driving?

Perception: Idioms, phrasals, culture clues

Idioms in context: Listen to the dialog below and underline any unfamiliar terms.

Carol: I don't know what to do! Our party plans are ruined!

Lori: Why? What happened?

Carol: Well, you know we were going to host a surprise bridal shower for Julia, but now everything is **on hold**.

Lori: Did someone **spill the beans**?

Carol: No. Worse! Steve and Julia **scrapped their plans** to be married!

Lori: You're kidding! I can't believe it!

Carol: Apparently Steve **got cold feet** and decided he wasn't ready for **the big leap**. He thinks Julia is expecting **castles in the air**, and he can't deliver them.

Lori: Can't they just **talk it out**? Marriage is never **a piece of cake**, but good honest communication can make all the difference in the world.

Carol: I know. Bob and I have had our ups and downs along the way. But when we run into a conflict, we **go back to the drawing board** and make **a new game plan**.

Lori: Things will work out. It just takes time, patience, and plenty of love. A little laughter never hurts, either.

Carol: Chuck Swindoll once said, "We are all faced with a series of great opportunities brilliantly disguised as impossible situations." That really impressed me. Maybe Bob can have a talk with Steve and encourage him and Julia **to talk things over**.

Lori: I'll talk to Julia, too. Actually, I'm embarrassed that I was more upset about the party than about Steve's and Julia's relationship. Hopefully, we'll hear some good news in the near future about them. I guess it's better **to deal with this head on** than to get married and discover major differences. It's always better **to nip problems in the bud.**

Lori: I agree. I do hope Steve and Julia will at least try talking out their differences. They seem like such a great couple!

New expressions:

Idioms:

What do you think these might mean?
How can you use them in your own conversations?

on hold	the big leap	go back to the drawing board
spill the beans	castles in the air	a new game plan
scrapped their plans	talk it out	talk things over
got cold feet	a piece of cake	deal with this head on
		nip problems in the bud

Phrasals and collocations: time, plans, future, make

run out of time	bright future
waste time	near future
save time	bleak future
have time	bright outlook

ambitious plans	make plans
audacious plans	make progress
grandiose plans	make trouble
long-term plans	make peace
ingenious plans	make a mistake
retirement plans	make an effort

Culture clues: Future orientation

Unlike some societies that greatly value the past and traditions, Americans as a whole tend to emphasize the future with its potential for greater success and happiness. Consequently, planning, setting goals, and working on projects play important roles in daily life.

The following is a quote from Alan Dundes' article published in 1969 by the George Washington Institute for Ethnographic Research:
> "Numerous proverbs, greetings, folk metaphors and other traditional oral formulas seem to reveal both a penchant for looking ahead and a reluctance to look back…Past oriented societies have myths (set in the past) while Americans have science fiction (set in the future)."

1. Observe conversations among your peers. Would you say that most topics seem to involve the past or the future?
2. How frequently during the day do you find yourself thinking about the future?
3. What are the advantages and disadvantages of future orientation?
4. How could future orientation be a motivator to academic success?

Listening and Bible Knowledge

Listening: Self-help tools

The internet provides almost endless tools for you to develop the English skills most problematic to you. There are interactive exercises for listening, speaking, pronunciation, presentations, accent reduction, and much more.

    a. Explore some of the web sites listed below (or others of your choosing) to discover those that could benefit you personally.

        www.ezslang.com
        www.headsupenglish.com
        www.englishstudydirect.com
        www.trainyouraccent.com

      (1) Plan to spend a minimum of 15 minutes a day working on problem areas via the internet. Then DO it! "Plan your work and work your plan."
      (2) Research sites that address your most pressing English problems. Invest time in using these resources to help you become more like a native English speaker.

    b. Develop relationships with native English speakers. Spend time interacting with them as often as possible. Enlist their help if you are comfortable doing that.

c. Watch English TV news, movies, DVDs. Listen to English radio programs. The more you immerse yourself in English, the more easily you will identify your problems and be able to address them specifically. Take the initiative to hear and use English as often as possible.

 Bible Knowledge

Part 1: Christ's Return to Heaven

After Jesus' resurrection, He arranged to meet His disciples on a mountain in Galilee, where He had begun His teaching ministry. During this gathering the disciples questioned Jesus about future events. Rather than outlining the future, Christ outlined His assignment for them: be His witnesses in Jerusalem, Judea, Samaria, and to the ends of the earth (Acts 1:8). More specifically, Christ said:

"All authority has been given Me in heaven and on earth. Go therefore and make disciples of all the nations, baptizing them in the name of the Father and of the Son and of the Holy Spirit, teaching them to observe all things that I have commanded you; and lo, I am with you always, even to the end of the age."

(Matthew 28:19, 20, NKJV)

He instructed His followers to remain in Jerusalem until they received the power of the Holy Spirit. Then, as He blessed them, Christ ascended into heaven while they watched. An angel appeared and reminded the startled disciples that just as Christ was taken up into heaven, so He would return.

After Jesus ascended into heaven, He sat at the right hand of God His disciples took their assignment seriously, and after receiving the Holy Spirit (recorded in Acts 2), they went everywhere preaching the good news of repentance and faith in the Lord Jesus Christ. The book of Acts summarizes the birth of the church, the work of the disciples, the persecution they experienced, and the start of local churches in Jerusalem, Judea, Samaria, and many other parts of the world. That global mission is still going on today.

 **Discussion: Part 1**

1. What was Jesus' assignment for His followers?
2. How is that being completed today?
3. Where did Jesus go after He left earth?
4. What does the biblical book of Acts tell us about the disciples' work?

Part 2: Christ's Promised Return and Future Events

The New Testament consists of the four Gospels—Matthew, Mark, Luke, and John, which record the birth, life, death, resurrection, and ascension of Christ; followed by the Book of Acts—an exciting history of the birth and growth of the early church, the Epistles—letters to local churches and pastors, and Revelation—a summary of future events leading up to Christ's return, the final defeat of Satan, judgment on all people, and the establishment of a new heaven and new earth. Christians believe that these writings are inspired of God and are His message for all people of all generations everywhere.

The epistles and pastoral letters include instruction for understanding God's plan for godly living; discerning truth from error; developing healthy relationships, love, faith, self-discipline, priorities. They provide all that man needs to know about the holy, perfect Creator God, about our own sin and its consequences, and how we can be restored to a relationship with God that He had intended at creation.

Scattered throughout these books are glimpses of future events, the culmination of history as we know it, and the return of Christ to reign as King of kings and Lord of lords. Jesus Christ is the Promised Deliverer who will keep His word and do all that He has planned. For the believer there is tremendous hope based not on wishes or maybes but on the sure Word of God. For those who refuse to trust Christ, there is judgment and eternal punishment for their own pride and sins.

Following is a brief summary of some of the future events described in Scripture.
* Jesus mentioned that there would be
    - False messiahs (deliverers)
    - Wars and rumors of wars
    - Famines and earthquakes in many places
    - Persecution of Christians
    - Preaching of the gospel to all nations

* While these things are happening, Christ's followers are to
    - Be content with the basics of life
    - Pursue righteousness, faith, love
    - Live blamelessly until Christ returns
* The Lord Himself will return from heaven with
    - A loud shout
    - The voice of the archangel
    - A trumpet call
    - The resurrection of dead believers, joined by living believers
* The Day of the Lord will come
    - Suddenly, as a thief in the night
    - While scoffers are ridiculing
    - While believers are anticipating this day

* Special events will follow
    - The wedding feast joining Christ (the groom) with the church (the bride)
    - The thousand year reign of Christ as King of kings and Lord of lords
    - The final defeat of Satan, who will be cast into the lake of fire forever
    - The judgment in which every individual will personally stand before God
    - Eternal rewards for those who are Christ's followers
    - Eternal punishment for those who have rejected Christ as Deliverer (Savior)
* Finally, the Creator God will bring about
    - A new heaven and a new earth—a world of peace and righteousness
    - The New Jerusalem where the glory of God will be its light
    - The collective worship of people from every nation, tribe, and people group
    - The end forever of tears, death, mourning, crying, and pain

At the conclusion of the book of Revelation, the Lord said to John,

> "I, Jesus, am the Alpha and Omega, the Beginning and the End, the root and offspring of David and the bright and morning star. Behold, I am coming soon. Blessed is he who keeps the word of the prophecy in this book; but I warn anyone not to add to this book or to take away from this book of prophecy."

John said, "Amen! Come, Lord Jesus." With John, believers in Christ are awaiting the return of the Promised Deliverer, the Lamb of God who takes away the sin of the world.

Discussion: Part 2

1. What are some signs that will happen before Jesus' return to earth?
2. Explain how we should live while waiting for Christ's return.
3. What is the blessed hope for people who die?
4. How does the analogy of "a thief in the night" fit with the return of Christ?
5. What is Satan's final destiny?
6. How did Christ define Himself to John? How can He be both?
7. What is your attitude about Jesus' return? Are you ready? Are you eager?

Assignment

1. Contemplating the future is common. Read the following quotes by some famous writers. Select one quote and use that as the basis for a poem or essay.

    George Will: "The future has a way of arriving unannounced."

    C.S. Lewis: "The future is something which everyone reaches at the rate of sixty minutes an hour, whatever he does, whoever he is."

    Abraham Lincoln: "The best thing about the Future is that it only comes one day at a time."

    Alex Haley: "In every conceivable manner, the family is link to our past, bridge to our future."

2. Watch the DVD "Left Behind." What is your impression of it? How does it compare with the biblical accounts of future events? If you are interested, there are two sequels: "Tribulation Force," and "World at War."

3. Draw or paint what you think a perfect world would look like. Perhaps you'd like to write a poem or description as well.

4. Study the following pictures. Then write an imaginary conversation between the people in each scene.

"Breaking Home Ties" by N. Rockwell

"Looking Out to Sea" by N. Rockwell

5. The return of Christ and the assurance of heaven have inspired many Christian hymn writers. One of the most widely sung and played is "Amazing Grace."
    a. Read the music below and listen to it via the internet if possible. Write any questions it brings to your mind.
    b. Research or ask your teacher for copies of these hymns relating to future events:
        * All Glory, Laud, and Honor
        * Jesus is Coming Again
        * One Day When Heaven

6. The Bible Knowledge sections of this book have be designed to give you an overall view of Christian belief as found in the Bible. Perhaps it has generated questions in your mind. Perhaps you'd like to learn more about certain aspects of Christian thought. Write your questions, then discuss them with your teacher. Feel free to request additional resources to assist you in understanding God's narrative for the nations.

Amazing Grace

175

Made in the USA
San Bernardino,
CA